Lucky Journey
Surviving Pancreatic Cancer

AUDREY GREENBLATT

This book is dedicated to Dr. Alan Kadet, the internist, who has been with us from the beginning, to Dr. Fadi Attiyeh, the surgeon, who saved Irwin's life, to Dr. Robert L. Fine, the research oncologist, who continues to give Irwin hope, and to Dawn Tsushima who has shown Irwin a new way to live.

Our Lucky Journey began on February 13, 2013, when my husband Irwin was diagnosed with pancreatic cancer.

You may wonder how lucky and cancer are related at all, but this story will document and explain the good and the bad, the sadness and the joy, and our hope of rejuvenation after heartache. For Irwin and me, our sons and son-in-law, our family and friends, it was the worst of times and the best of times, although we didn't always know it.

You will meet with the doctors, nurses, and staff who became so important to us. You will experience the grueling, systematic, scary process of choosing the right doctors and deciding the best hospital for the seven-hour Whipple surgery and for the postoperative six-month chemotherapy protocol. Our **Lucky Journey** will ask you to travel with us through the painful, difficult, humiliating, and debilitating side effects as we finally move from darkness into sunlight and recuperation.

We will travel forward together, as you walk in our shoes and learn about the many emotional and psychological changes that Irwin and I experienced during this life-altering time. Everyday words such as caregiver, superman, courage, fine, God, oy vey, shit, strength, feel, fuck, heartache, anger, and many others will take on a new and deeper meaning. Phrases like "You can say pancreatic cancer and lucky in the same sentence," "It's not over until it's over," and "How much more can I take?" will become part of your language.

Our **Lucky Journey** will not end until, like me, you have learned what it means "to give back" by sharing moments of sorrow, joy, hope, support, and encouragement with others. Perhaps you will experience, as Irwin did, your own metamorphosis!

TABLE OF CONTENTS

1

WE DIDN'T ASK FOR THIS

We didn't ask for this, and we certainly didn't want it. Nobody asks for this, and certainly nobody wants it. But when a diagnosis of pancreatic cancer is given, you and your family's lives are forever changed. Everyone knows or hears about people fighting cancer, and they feel sorry and sympathetic for the victim's plight, but people go on with their own lives, and that is as it should be.

Our story is personal and explains how our lives changed on February 13, 2013, at 5:00 p.m. I am writing this story to document our journey and to explain the good and the bad, the joy and the sadness, the love and the devotion, and the hope of rejuvenation after heartache. For Irwin and me, our two sons, our son-in-law, and our family and friends, it was the worst of times and also the best of times, although we didn't always realize it. I will begin at the beginning.

I have known Irwin for fifty years. We met when we were both seventeen at a party on October 19, 1962. I was a senior in high school, and Irwin was a freshman in college. I was a short, fat, plain girl and was so happy that a "college man" would talk to me.

I had just seen a Cary Grant movie, where he said to some young, blond plaything, "Would you like to see my etchings?" to lure her to his bedroom. So, to be clever, I said to Irwin, "I'm an artist. Would you like to see my etchings?"

He thought that etchings meant breasts, so excitedly he said, "Sure." And that was how we started.

Our story continued in the1960s. We were of the generation when people protested the war in Vietnam; women burned their bras; and many used drugs, which were available to the masses, and smoked pot as their rite of passage. That was not our story. We married at twenty to avoid Irwin being drafted, and we both worked hard to save money to buy our first home for $17,000. We had a son, and then two years later, our second son was born. We knew people who partied but not around us. We were nerdy, but we thought we were pretty fabulous. We had costume parties, Academy Award celebrations, and Love Boat parties. Forty close friends looked forward to our special events when disco was queen. We would roll up the rug and dance the night away, as Donna Summers's voice came through the eight-track, while our sons looked on in disbelief. I was a spectacular cook and entertainer, a caring and involved mom, and a hardworking and loving wife.

We opened Delaware Valley High School- Student Education Center, a small private school, and worked together with at-risk students for thirty years. Our school kept us busy eleven months out of the year. We enjoyed the good life. As part of this good life, however, we never smoked or drank much and lived a healthy lifestyle. I had been overweight my entire life but in September of 1989, when Darren our younger son left for college, I attended Weight Watchers and lost seventy pounds; I have kept it off to this day. We traveled on cruises and took trips to Europe with our sons over the past fifty years. We bought a beautiful home in the suburbs, which had a great school district.

The boys thrived, had many friends, went to college, and pursued their own interests, hobbies, and lifestyles. We were accepting and open and encouraged them and their friends and also our students at school to be good citizens and to never take advantage of others as they climbed their ladders of success. We had a comfortable life, worked hard, and were good people. Our two wonderful sons each have a beautiful daughter: Maya is eight years old, and Olive is three. Olive has two daddies in a contemporary "modern family."

We sold our school in 1999, retired to New York City, and never looked back. Now in hindsight we realize that this city and its incredible medical facilities, doctors, and nurses saved Irwin's life.

On Tuesday, February 12, 2013, Irwin fainted at school, where he was teaching. He was unconscious for less than a minute. The school nurse, Lisa assumed it was his diabetes. That night he had intense back and stomach pains for hours. We hardly slept. I looked on the Internet to see what could cause this kind of pain and came up with a possible diagnosis of pancreatitis. I called my sister Barbara and told her the symptoms. She was my go-to medical person and knew a great deal of information. She should have been a doctor, which is a story for another time. I begged Irwin to go to the emergency room at St. Luke-Roosevelt Hospital across the street from where we lived, but he refused.

At 6:30 a.m. we dressed and took a taxi, the few shorts blocks, to see our primary physician, Dr. Alan Kadet, who saw patients without appointments starting at 7:00 a.m. Irwin was in so much pain that when Dr. Kadet felt his belly, he nearly jumped off of the exam table. I told Dr. Kadet that I thought it was pancreatitis, and he said in his humorous way, "Thank you, Dr. Greenblatt." Dr. Kadet called ahead to St. Luke's-Roosevelt Hospital and arranged for Irwin to see Dr. Cajulis immediately. We hopped into a taxi and arrived at the hospital in five minutes.

2

THE BOMB HITS US

In the emergency room at St. Luke's-Roosevelt Hospital, we saw everything: stabbing victims, heart attacks, and people in distress of all kinds. The man in the area next to ours, separated only by a curtain, had eaten too much and wanted an enema. He was so large he couldn't find his own rectum. We laughed just to break the tension. Irwin was taken to an area for a CAT scan, blood work, and a cardiogram. His pain had not subsided. He was given pain medication but to no avail. The enema man left, and then a diabetic man was carried into the area next to ours. He had passed out on the subway platform and was brought to the hospital by ambulance. The doctors tried to regulate his sugar, but he was not happy because the medics had cut his shirt and pants to treat him on the subway platform and he was upset because he had to catch a train home. He was so insistent that he pulled the IV out while in the emergency room and shouted at anyone who would listen to his complaints. He finally felt better and left. So again we laughed at the show going on around us and how trite people could be.

It was 5:00 p.m. when I was called to the nurses' station. We had been in the emergency room cubicle since 8:00 a.m. Dr. Kadet was on the phone and wanted to speak to me. This wasn't a good omen. He said hello and told me in a quiet voice that Irwin had pancreatic cancer. I couldn't believe I was hearing these words. I shook.

I couldn't breathe and asked, "Are you telling me Irwin has pancreatic cancer?"

His answer was, "Yes." This wonderful, kind, smart doctor who had known us for ten years had to tell me this devastating news, and now I had to tell Irwin. Irwin was twenty feet away from where I was standing, and it seemed like a mile. I watched myself from a distance. As if in a movie, as I walked to Irwin's bed, I thought that this couldn't be real, but to my horror it was.

My sister Barbara and I had always joked whenever any medical problem developed, "As long as they didn't diagnose pancreatic cancer, then it can be managed." It was our motto in life. Well, now I had to tell Irwin this awful news, and the reality was overwhelming. "Irwin, I have very bad news. You have pancreatic cancer." There was no way to sugarcoat it. We both started to cry.

Irwin blurted out, "I'm only sixty-seven, and I don't want to die."

What could I say? I responded, putting up a brave front, "We'll fight this," but in my heart I was so scared. Even as I write this now, months later, I cry as I relive those frightening moments.

I couldn't believe that this was happening. Irwin said, "Who will smell your pants?" I lost my sense of taste and smell fifteen years earlier, so Irwin, who has always had a super nose, always smelled my pants so I knew when to wash them. We laughed and cried again. "Call the kids," he said. How do you break this kind of news? I had called our sons earlier in the morning and told them that Irwin was in the hospital with severe pain, but this was something else entirely, an incomprehensible nightmare!

I called our son in Philadelphia, and he was quiet and in shock. Then I called our son Darren at Donna Bell's Bake Shop, which he owned with business partner, Matthew Sandusky, and actress Pauley Perrette, located in New York City.

He said, "I'm coming to the hospital," but Irwin said he couldn't see anyone then. I arranged to meet Darren and his partner, Sam, in the hospital lobby to walk me home.

Then I called Barbara, and I told her. She started to wail and shout.

Fred, her husband, screamed, "What's wrong?"

After Barbara told him, Irwin and I in the hospital emergency room, and Barbara and Fred at home sobbed on the phone. Barbara said that she would call Carol and Ronnie, my other sisters, but I couldn't allow her to do so. This was my job today. So, crying, I called each of them, and then we all cried again. They had known Irwin for fifty years and, let's face it, this was a bad cancer. I called Marty, Irwin's brother, and Ruth, his wife, and they were also in shock. One of their closest friends had been diagnosed with this dreaded disease and was undergoing treatment because her tumor was inoperable, and she was not doing well.

A wonderful social worker spoke to us in our cubicle and suggested that we get other opinions. She also gave us some information and phone numbers for support groups. Several male nurses who had been attending Irwin since he had been admitted that morning (could it be that this morning was only ten hours ago?) were so kind and told us not to give up hope.

The nurses moved Irwin to a regular room, and I took his belongings with us. In the elevator we saw Gayle King (Oprah's friend). I said hi to her as if I knew her personally.

Once Irwin was settled, I said good-bye and met Darren and Sam in the lobby. The three of us were crying messes as we walked down Fifty-Eighth Street to my apartment one block from the hospital. They hadn't eaten, and neither had I. We sat around my dining room table and talked about what we could do. They ate between tears. I had no appetite. After they left I became hysterical. With one call our lives had changed. I turned on the TV as a distraction and saw that Bonnie Franklin had died of pancreatic cancer at sixty-nine. My world was crashing down around me.

The phone rang off the hook. Ruth and Marty tried to be helpful by suggesting that we visit Memorial Sloan Kettering, the world-renowned cancer hospital, for another opinion.

I tried to sleep, but sobbed into the pillow. I slept a little and sobbed a lot. I prayed and talked to God, my parents, Irwin's mom, and my special Aunt Dee, all of whom had died years ago. "Please help us. Please, God, there must be an answer." This couldn't be the end. I had always prayed at night before I went to sleep since my father died twenty-eight years earlier. I believed something (God, or some inexplicable force) was listening, and I prayed for hope. "Please, God, just give us hope." Each time I woke up to pee, I sobbed and prayed. Hope, hope, please! It was like being in a bad dream.

I woke up at 6:00 a.m. and gave Madison, our cat, some food and an insulin shot. This had been Irwin's job, but now it was mine. Our new reality! I went to the hospital, but visiting hours didn't start until 10:00 a.m. so I returned home and cried again and again. I met Darren at ten, and we walked to the hospital and visited Irwin. All of us sobbed.

Then Dr. Barbara Wexelman came into Irwin's room. She said that his tumor was operable and that her associate Dr. Fadi Attiyeh was an expert in this kind of surgery, called a Whipple procedure. Dr. Attiyeh's name was familiar because he had operated on me twelve years earlier for a benign tumor on my kidney. Dr. Wexelman said it was *bashert*, the Jewish word for *kismet* (meant to be). She said, "If my parents needed this operation, Dr. Attiyeh would be my first and only choice." That was the good news. The bad news was that Dr. Attiyeh was in Lebanon (not Pennsylvania) for a week and wasn't expected back until February 25, two weeks later.

So at least there was some direction and hope. Then to our surprise, ten minutes later, Dr. Attiyeh walked into the room. Early morning sunlight streamed in and surrounded Dr. Attiyeh as he entered through the door. It was like Jesus walking on a cloud. He shook my hand and said that he remembered our family from my previous operation. Then he took both of Irwin's hands firmly into his and said, "I looked at all of your scans and tests, and the tumor is in the head of the pancreas—the best place. It looks encapsulated, and I can operate." He continued, "You won't be connected the way you were when you were born, and your insides will be different, but you will be fine!" Being able to have the Whipple surgery was absolutely crucial to Irwin's situation. It gave him the opportunity to live...because without it, Irwin probably would die within the year. If the tumor were one inch down closer to the tail of the pancreas, then surgery would not be an option. Never had one inch ever meant so much.

We stared at each other with incredible thankfulness and amazement. Dr. Attiyeh took out his cell phone and looked at his calendar. He was leaving for Lebanon the next day and would return on the twenty-fifth and would operate on February 26. He told Irwin to fatten up because he would lose weight after surgery. Then he quietly and quickly left the room the way he had entered it as if by magic. Irwin, Darren, and I cried for joy. There was hope, everything I had prayed for. Hope, tears, prayers—such simple everyday words!

We didn't need other opinions, and there would be no additional calling for appointments. We had a surgeon whom we knew from twelve years earlier. We had a surgery date in less than two weeks, and we had hope. In less than eighteen hours from that devastating diagnosis, we had a plan. We said we would not allow negativity into our lives. We would surround ourselves with positive people, and we would only think in terms of getting through the next eleven days until the Whipple could be performed.

Irwin was released from the hospital with his bag of pain-controlling pills. We were going home to fatten him up before surgery. We didn't worry about his diabetes sugar numbers, which in hindsight had been our first clue of a problem. Since the previous August, Irwin's sugar numbers jumped from the normal 120 to more than 300 or more for no apparent reason. He had always watched his diet, ate little or no carbs, no sweets or anything high in sugar. When his numbers went crazy, he was so frustrated because there was no explanation. So he cut back on his normal food and lost five pounds, going from 131 to 126 pounds, and he was irritable and angry all of the time.

His first endocrinologist sat behind a computer screen and asked what Irwin thought the problem was. He never looked up from his laptop and never touched or examined Irwin. The doctor adjusted Irwin's medications, but there was no improvement. After two months we found a different endocrinologist, who thought Irwin had type 1.5 diabetes (adult-onset childhood diabetes) and put him on injectable insulin. Again there were no appreciable improvements. It was already mid-January, five months since the glucose sugar numbers started rising. We argued over seeing another endocrinologist, but Irwin felt defeated and said, "Why bother?"

I kept repeating, "It's not what you're eating. Maybe there's a problem with your pancreas." Thank you, Dr. Greenblatt!

Then on February 12, 2013, when Irwin fainted while at school, it became obvious that something was indeed wrong with the pancreas. When Irwin was in the hospital, the second endocrinologist stopped by to see him. He said, "I guess we should have done a simple blood test, and that would have indicated a pancreas problem." We didn't take time to point the finger and to blame because we only wanted to think in a positive way.

Irwin planned to be home during this hiatus week until the Whipple could be performed, but didn't have the correct pain medication and was in excruciating pain. I was at school, so Darren took a taxi from the bake shop and then called 911 and had an ambulance take Irwin back to the hospital on Friday morning, less than twenty-four hours since he had been released on Thursday. He had to stay ahead of the pain with regulated meds. With pancreatic cancer it was very unusual to have had pain until it was too late. Luckily for Irwin pancreatic pain saved his life before the cancer could spread from the head down that crucial inch toward the tail.

The week before the surgery passed slowly. I taught school, and Irwin stayed home, trying to eat, rest, and gain strength before the big day. The medication kept the pain under control. We returned to the hospital on Sunday, February 24, and were told that the surgery had to be postponed until Thursday, February 28, because the special operating room that Dr. Attiyeh used for the seven-hour operation wasn't available. Rather than return home, he was kept at the hospital to monitor and control the pain and to give him the much needed rest that was required before this severe operation.

While in the hospital before the operation, Irwin was in a room with a drug-addicted patient. When this man heard that Irwin had been receiving oxycodone, he screamed, "I want fucking oxy," over and over again. There was no sleeping for Irwin that night. The next day he was moved to another room. This time the roommate was only nuts, but his bed was near the window so he controlled the heat. The room was like a sauna, the blinds were closed, and the TV volume was turned high all night. The next day Irwin's room was changed again. This time his elderly roommate was so abusive to the nurses that we were angered. This patient complained that the food was shit, that he had been a cook in the navy during World War II, and that the navy threw away better food than what was being offered in the hospital. We never complained about the food; in fact, we thought it was tasty!

Irwin was nervous and exhausted, and he counted down the days to Thursday. However, both of us were very positive because we were so lucky to be able to have a Whipple operation, which could save Irwin's life. A mere inch farther down into the pancreas would have meant no surgery and a death sentence. The inconvenience of hospital roommates became unimportant.

I saw Irwin on Wednesday evening, the night before the surgery. We talked, joked, laughed, and cried. I said, "Everything will be fine. We have a wonderful doctor, whom we have known and have faith in. Think positive, and we will get through this."

Irwin said, "I am ready and relieved that the time has come."

"I'll see you after surgery," were my parting words as I kissed him goodbye.

3

DR. ATTIYEH AND DR. WHIPPLE

I was at the hospital during the day, every day, and then went home at night to return phone calls. Everyone wanted to hear the latest information. It had been two weeks since diagnosis, but it seemed like a lifetime of emotional, psychological, and physical upheaval in our lives.

The day of the surgery, Darren and Sam and Marty, Irwin's brother, and his wife, Ruth, were at the hospital. My sister Ronnie took the train from Baltimore, Maryland, and my sister Barbara took the train from Trenton, New Jersey. I was told not to arrive at the hospital until around eleven o'clock. Irwin was to be prepped at 7:00 for the seven-hour surgery, and we would not be able to see him before surgery. I met Darren, Ronnie, and Barb for breakfast at 9:30. We were nervous and frightened and had no appetite. Ruth called at 9:35 and asked why I wasn't at the hospital. I explained that I was told not to get there until eleven. We quickly finished breakfast paid the check and went to the hospital.

Marty greeted me with, "You look awful!" and I probably did—but how was I supposed to look? I wasn't going to a party! Our nerves were on edge, and I was frightened, worried, and nervous. What if Dr. Attiyeh came from surgery and told us that he found more than he had anticipated and that he couldn't remove the tumor? We were told that Irwin was late being taken down to the operating room, and we wouldn't know anything for hours. The time dragged on.

At 1:30 Dr. Attiyeh looked for us in the waiting room. Darren and I asked hesitantly, "How did everything go?" I had prayed the night before for no surprises, and those were Dr. Attiyeh's first words: "No surprises." The operation went better than expected and was completed in five hours, not the usual seven. Such wonderful news! Ruth asked the doctor if Irwin would need chemo or radiation. Dr. Attiyeh said, "It is too soon to know." We thanked him, and then we hugged each other and cried with happiness.

We crossed the street and had lunch at the Greek Kitchen. We ate like pigs from relief that the operation was over and that the long, very involved surgery was over. Half of Irwin's stomach, part of the digestive system, the gallbladder, part of the pancreas and the tumor, and bile ducts had been removed and what was left had been reconnected successfully.

Dr. Allen Whipple, the son of Presbyterian missionaries, was born in 1881 in Iran. When he originally performed this surgery in the 1930s, the patient had to be left open for two full days in order to complete the operation. In 1940 Dr. Whipple was able to shorten the process to one day. During his lifetime he performed thirty-seven pancreaticoduodenectomies. His brilliance saved lives when there was no hope.

We walked back to the hospital to visit Irwin in intensive care. Dr. Craig Forleiter, an ICU doctor, gave us an update. He told us that Irwin was doing amazingly well, and even joked that he just couldn't go out drinking with the doctor that night. Darren brought a large box of Donna Bell's pastries from the bake shop he owned to help thank the staff. Dr. Craig said, "I bake to relax from the pressures of ICU," and showed us pictures of his homemade challah and cheese crackers on his phone. More importantly he told us that there were clear margins around the removed tumor (that the tissues surrounding the tumor were cancer-free) and that all looked good.

Darren and I were the first to see Irwin. He was alert and smiling, happy that the surgery was over. The intensive care nurses were at his beck and call. Ruth and Marty visited him next. They thought he looked wonderful. Then Barb, Ronnie, and Sam had their turns. We all met in the waiting area and cried and hugged one another. All of the visitors left by five o'clock. Irwin was heavily medicated, but his spirits were flying. We all went home knowing that he was in good hands.

I had several calls to make. I hadn't told very many people before the surgery. It was too exhausting, heartbreaking, and emotional to have to repeat the story over and over. The handful of close friends and family that I told stopped breathing for a moment when I said the words *pancreatic cancer.*

I had to comfort them and tell them to breathe and that I believed that this would all turn out well. I felt tremendous pressure to be strong. I called our son in Philadelphia and my sister Carol, who were unable to be at the hospital. They offered words of encouragement and support, and Carol told a story about someone she knew who was a seven-year Whipple surgery survivor and doing very well.

Only 20 percent of all pancreatic cancer patients could have the Whipple surgery because 80 percent of these pancreatic cancerous tumors were inoperable. After surgery, chemo and/or radiation were usually required. I felt that because Irwin was lucky enough to be in the 20 percent; that we had known Dr. Attiyeh, and that this surgery was the doctor's specialty; that we lived across the street from the hospital; that we had a surgery date within eighteen hours of diagnosis; and that we hadn't wasted valuable time getting appointments for second and third opinions with other surgeons and hospitals—all these things gave us hope.

Hope!

We would deal with whatever would come next with no negativity, and only positive thoughts, relief, and joy.

I walked home with Darren and Sam, a far cry from the way we walked home two weeks ago. Irwin had survived the surgery and was doing really well. I entered our apartment, fed Madison, gave him his shot and then I burst into tears of relief. Tonight I hopefully would sleep like a baby get some needed rest, because tomorrow was another day.

Our son from Philadelphia and Stephanie, his girlfriend at the time, arrived the next day, Friday, and we were all amazed with Irwin's progress. He was out of bed—no kidding—walked a little, and was hungry. He was not permitted food yet. His insides had been rearranged. Part of his pancreas, part of the digestive system, half of his stomach, his gallbladder, some liver bile ducts, and several feet of intestines had been removed, and then everything that was left had been reconnected; all his parts had to heal and calm down, and then slowly food would be reintroduced.

Stephanie was in charge of a nursing practice in Philadelphia and had assisted during Whipple surgeries; she was an invaluable source of information and support for our family. God sent us an angel when we needed one. She said that she couldn't believe Irwin was doing so well; she called him Superman and me Wonder Woman. She told us that we needed to be strong and that the road ahead was really a mountain. Stephanie's reinforcing strength, important explanations, suggestions for Irwin's care, and positive attitude helped us so much during those difficult days.

Saturday, March 2, only two days from surgery, Irwin was doing so well that he was moved from intensive care to a postop floor. By noon, I was with Irwin as they settled him into his new room. However, by one o'clock, his pain was so severe that I called a nurse from the nurses' station. She said that he was receiving pain meds and that he would have to be patient until they kicked in. We waited fifteen minutes—which seemed like hours—and by then Irwin was screaming in pain. He squeezed my hand so hard that it felt broken. I saw the nurse again and reminded her that it had been an hour with no relief.

Sam stopped by, and I told him to go back to the intensive care unit and tell those nurses about our current situation. Of course that created a problem, because once Irwin had left intensive care, he was no longer their patient. Then Irwin's floor nurse walked into the room and shouted at me for overstepping the rules. I felt like the actress Shirley MacLaine in the film *Terms of Endearment.*

Frustrated, I roared, "Don't yell at me. My husband has been in increasing excruciating pain." And then I started to cry.

Very shaken, I called Dr. Attiyeh directly. He returned my call within minutes. Finally a doctor appeared and gave Irwin meds that brought some relief. For five hours, he had suffered unbearable pain. Perhaps he was moved too quickly out of intensive care.

Irwin wanted me to stay at the hospital that night. There was a lounge across the hall from his room. They only had chairs and no recliners. I turned on the TV to a *Law and Order* marathon and fell asleep. I woke up to pee at least three times during the night and checked Irwin each time to make sure that he was pushing his meds pump; then I went back to my chair and the TV. This worked well. He was comfortable, and I slept as much as I normally did. It had been an emotionally and physically exhausting day. I learned the hard way that in a hospital, you must be your own best advocate, do what has to be done, make quick decisions, and not be afraid to shout if necessary—and that sometimes tears and crying help!

In the morning after I checked Irwin, I went home, gave the cat a shot of insulin, fed him, showered, changed clothes, and went back to the hospital. Irwin's pain had been managed. He was hungry, but no food was permitted until the next day. So instead, we talked about food and what he'd eat when he was able to. First, egg foo young and shrimp lo mein. Then, pizza. He hadn't had an appetite since August, almost six months earlier. This was fun and a welcome change.

On Monday Irwin had clear broth and Jell-O. The pain was under control, but he felt the need to move his bowels. The pain meds had constipated him, and there had been no food in his system for five days. He was able to tolerate the food, and because of his strength, was told that he might be able to go home the next day. The roommates had been intolerable, so he felt happy to anticipate having his own bed to look forward to. The total post-operative stay was five days, rather than the normal two weeks. It seemed that Irwin was truly becoming Superman...and then there was joy in our world.

The day was Tuesday, March 5, exactly three weeks since Irwin had passed out at school. He ate solid food and felt great. We saw our wonderful caring Dr. Craig, who made a special trip from ICU to see how Irwin was progressing. A rare human being.

We took a taxi home even though the hospital was across the street from our apartment. Just getting him into the taxi was excruciating, but Irwin was going home and we were thrilled.

Being together for fifty years, there had been rough spots, patches where we thought our marriage was crazy. There were issues, differences, and problems, but our real values and strengths held strong, especially during difficult hard times. Irwin took a nap, and then for our first post-hospital dinner, he ate soup and an egg salad sandwich. He could only eat tiny portions and did so often during the day. Many thanks to Donna Bell's Bake Shop, and Matthew, baker extrodinarre, who showed his love and support through generously sending food home for us and the hospital staff.

The next morning started out good. Irwin's strength was returning, but his weight unfortunately had dropped to a new low of 110 pounds. By noon the pain had returned. The oxy had caused him to be constipated. He was doubled over in pain.

We called Dr. Attiyeh, and he said, "Stop the oxy, now! Use extra-strength Tylenol." Cold turkey. I bought stool softeners and an enema kit. His pain was an eleven on a scale of one to ten. I gave him an enema; however, nothing happened. This was like the bad day at the hospital when his meds hadn't kicked in. He couldn't find a place for himself to be comfortable. After an agonizing three hours, he finally went to the bathroom. He had been backed up since before the surgery. Too much information! The oxy had done him in. Why did people take this drug for "pleasure"? I didn't understand. How being constipated, which was a side effect of this drug, makes you feel good was a mystery to us.

Because Irwin left the hospital after only five days, he had five drains and container bags that needed to be emptied several times a day. I became a nurse and did what had to be done. I was a quick learner. Irwin was getting stronger and strengthening his position as super patient, and I was becoming a wonder woman in my own right. It wasn't pretty or easy, but we did what we had to do, and through it all we were thankful.

4

CHOOSING THE PROTOCOL

Irwin had an appointment to see Dr. Attiyeh to have his staples removed from the Whipple incision just below his ribs to his groin. At the office, Grace, the doctor's receptionist, was so kind. She told us that Irwin was a miracle patient. Normally after this surgery, a person was kept in the hospital for two weeks; however, Irwin was home in five days. This was a really difficult operation. Long ago when the Whipple was first attempted, the patient was surgically opened and kept open for two days because the doctor could not complete this very involved procedure in one day. We were anxious until Dr. Attiyeh discussed the lab results with us. The tumor was small, 3cm, encapsulated with clear margins, but there was one suspicious lymph node, so Dr. Attiyeh suggested chemo and radiation. In fact, because pancreatic cancer often returned to another part of the body, even after a Whipple operation, some kind of post-operative protocol was suggested.

Dr. Attiyeh was the boss, but we had been blindsided because we hadn't realized that other procedures would be necessary. We had learned a lot, but we had much more to learn. We were shocked that after all of the pain and suffering, Irwin's ordeal was not finished; in effect, he was just beginning again in a new phase. He had to face another ordeal. Dr. Attiyeh recommended an oncologist connected with Roosevelt Hospital, but the oncologist couldn't see us for two weeks. Irwin would have time to continue to rest and become stronger, and perhaps gain some weight. As a person who had always struggled with my weight, I couldn't imagine the luxury of being able to eat anything I wanted, as Irwin's instructions said, but of course, this command came at such a price.

School was closed for spring break. Irwin was anxious to get back to something normal, which for him was teaching. Whatever his motivation, it was his goal to be able to teach in April. We went to meet with the oncologist at the hospital on April 4. We were kept waiting for three hours. We were finally called in to see the doctor. Unfortunately, we first met with his assistant, who was a foreign gentleman whom we had difficulty understanding. He recorded vital information, and then we waited again.

The doctor, who finally entered the room, didn't know who we were, hadn't read the assistant's notes, and told us not to interrupt him with questions as he proceeded; then he gave us, by rote, his chemo protocol. It would last six months and also include two months of radiation on a daily basis. We were sick to our stomachs. This seemed excessive to us, but what did we know? He told us not to look on the Internet because it would only confuse us. He had been interrupted with cell phone calls the entire time we were with him. I thought that if everything was so good, why did Irwin need this kind of protocol? We told him that we would get another opinion. He said that was our right and that we could begin his treatment in two weeks.

We walked out of his office in disbelief and not happy with his demeanor. Our friend Arlene, who had undergone chemo protocols over the past ten years, had told us, "You must have confidence in your doctors because they will see you through the difficult time ahead; it is so important to feel a connection." We certainly didn't have it with this doctor. We knew that there was an answer somewhere and that we would find it.

When we got home, we spoke to our sons, our son-in-law, and especially Stephanie. Stephanie had so much medical knowledge and common sense. Stephanie said, "It is often the case that as a precaution, cancer patients need a chemo protocol after surgery. But don't forget, there are other hospitals." She had researched Columbia Presbyterian because it offered a multidisciplinary approach. She also suggested that we get several other opinions besides the one at Roosevelt.

I called Memorial Sloan Kettering Cancer Center for a second opinion and made an appointment for the following week. They required that the records from Roosevelt Hospital be released to them, as well as ten to fifteen slides from the surgery and a CD of the operation. We visited Roosevelt Hospital and arranged to have everything sent to Sloan. Returning to Roosevelt Hospital so soon after surgery reminded us of how lucky we were. The records we needed were stored in the basement of the building. As we tried to find our way there, we became lost in the serpentine never-ending halls. We finally found the room. The person at the desk was very friendly and helpful.

When we had spoken to Stephanie, she told us to speak to Kindra at the Pancreas Center at Columbia Presbyterian Hospital, where important research work was being done in pancreatic cancer. Dr. Robert Fine was in charge of an aggressive, progressive, experimental post-Whipple and chemotherapy protocol. Speaking to Kindra had a calming effect. She told us to send the slides and records from the surgery. We went back to the records department at Roosevelt Hospital for a second time in two days. Now we knew where to go, and we had new copies made and sent to Dr. Fine's office. Kindra called to say that Dr. Fine wanted additional blood work, an MRI, and a PET scan before we met with him. Our health insurance didn't want to cover the PET scan, but Dr. Fine convinced the insurance company that all the tests were necessary. He and Columbia Presbyterian Hospital were the only ones who required all of this additional information. They wanted the entire picture, which we also felt was very important.

Dr. Fine's office scheduled all of the blood work and scans that he required before he would meet with us. We arrived at Columbia Presbyterian Hospital for the blood work and MRI. Unfortunately the blood department could not find the orders. It was past five o'clock, and there were no people on the eighth floor, where the secretary Kindra's office was located. Irwin and I started to wander in the hospital's quiet deserted corridors looking for someone who might help us with the correct paperwork.

We looked down a long, dark, empty corridor, and someone with a kind voice said, "Can I help you?" We explained that Irwin was a Whipple survivor (like a secret password to a club we never wanted to join), and the man said, "I'll have the instructions sent down to hematology." A problem was resolved. The voice from the small office at the end of the dark corridor was that of Dr. Fine, although we didn't know it at the time. Nor did we realize the impact that this quiet, unassuming man would have on our lives in the future.

Previously Irwin had been claustrophobic, but with a Valium and some good advice from Arlene, our dear friend, he had the MRI with no problem.

I told him, "Close your eyes the minute you lie down and think about our little granddaughters and all the fun we had on the rental boat last summer." It worked like a charm. Dr. Fine didn't want to see us until he had the PET scan results, so that he could have a complete picture of Irwin's situation. Arlene again gave us step-by-step instructions on what Irwin should do to get through the PET scan. He was fine. At age sixty-eight, he had become a real pro at medical test taking. Irwin was showing more flexibility in his behavior as he dealt with his pancreatic cancer.

Our appointment with Memorial Sloan Kettering for our second opinion was Monday, April 29, at 9:00 a.m., and at Columbia Presbyterian for our third opinion at 2:00 p.m. on the same day. We were so lucky to live in New York City and to have world-renowned hospitals and doctors within our reach.

We hailed a taxi and arrived ten minutes later at Sloan. We waited in long lines to take the elevator to the proper floor, where the Chemo Lounge was located. There were at least one hundred people waiting. There was a waterfall and art sculptures, and peaceful music played in the background. We watched as patients were called in for their chemo infusions. Many were bald, with graying skin, sitting in wheelchairs. Would this be our future? We were upset, nervous, and frightened about the unknown. Irwin had come through one of the most difficult and involved delicate surgeries with great success. But now we faced an involved, many months-long chemo protocol with the possibility of devastating side effects.

We met with Dr. Yu, who was brilliant and knowledgeable regarding the latest technology. We appreciated his demeanor. Dr. Yu said to Irwin, "You do not need radiation because there is nothing to radiate." The tumor had been removed, and he recommended a mild chemo for six months. We were relieved about not needing radiation and realized that we now had a choice. We had waited two hours to see the doctor, but it had been worth the wait. We taxied home and talked about the day's events. No radiation!

Thank you, God! We had been impressed with Dr. Yu and felt that we could work with him and his hospital.

We grabbed a quick sandwich for lunch, then headed uptown on the A train (we were humming Duke Ellington's song "Take the A Train") to Columbia Presbyterian for our two o'clock appointment and our third and last interview. After all the testing had been completed as per Dr. Fine's request, it was now time for the visit with him and his staff to discuss the protocol.

We arrived at Columbia Presbyterian. Our destination only required three stops, less than fifteen minutes from home. The A-train runs express from Columbus Circle, our stop, to 125 Street and then145 Street and then 168 Street. The atmosphere was much less grand than Sloan—no waterfall, no artwork, and no new wave music. This hospital was older, plain but functional. On the wall there was a portrait of Dr. Whipple. How ironic! We felt at home. A dozen people were waiting, rather than one hundred.

Two hours passed very slowly until we were called in to see the doctor. His nurse, Dawn Tsushima, completed the intake. She was a large, sweet, granola kind of woman, so warm and welcoming, very down-to-earth, with deep blue eyes that showed compassion, depth, and understanding. She had the most wonderful things to say about Dr. Fine and his program. We now found out that when we were here the preceding week for the MRI and there had been a mix-up with the paperwork, it was Dr. Fine who had helped us that busy and at times overwhelming day. The quiet, unpretentious doctor in his small office at the end of a long hospital corridor who had helped us was the famous world-renowned research oncologist at Columbia Presbyterian Hospital. This was a reinforcing sign for Irwin and me. Dawn explained that she would be our nurse from day one until forever. She would see us every time we came to the hospital. She would always take our phone calls when we had a question or a problem. We would be people, not a number. We made our minds up at that moment. Dawn would be our advocate, friend, and the ultimate caregiver.

Dr. Fine had been in charge of a successful trial program for the last five years. During our visit he explained that 70 to 75 percent of all pancreatic tumors return in the liver or somewhere else when only mild chemo (Gemzar) was used. However, his progressive, aggressive, research-based protocol included three drugs, GXT (Gemzar, Xeloda, and Taxotere—with the Xeloda taken orally and the Gemzar and Taxotere by infusion). Two weeks on the chemo and then one week off, for a period of six months. Oral chemo meds every day for fourteen days, and then a four-hour chemo infusion once a week for two weeks. He explained that there was a shadow on Irwin's MRI, but the PET scan showed Irwin was cancer-free. What glorious words! If cancer had shown on the PET scan, Irwin would not have been eligible for this protocol, whose results over the years indicated a reduction in the return of cancer from 75 percent to 30 percent.

Dr. Fine spoke with us for an hour, and we felt honored to be accepted into his trial. We believed that Irwin would not have been accepted if Dr. Fine thought that he would slant the trials in a negative way. Dawn told us that this protocol would not be easy and that there would be challenges and many side effects, but we remembered when Dr. Attiyeh, the surgeon, said two months earlier, "You will be fine." Well, it was bashert again with Dr. Fine!

Our emotions were mixed: joy, happiness, encouragement, feelings of security, sunlight but also darkness, fear of the unknown and the what-if factor, and worry about how Irwin would react mentally, emotionally, and physically to a six-month severe chemo protocol—but in the end, we had a quiet feeling that everything would be "fine." Fine!

5

HE ISN'T SUPERMAN; HE JUST WANTS TO LIVE

The facts were simple: Irwin was diagnosed with pancreatic cancer, had survived Whipple surgery within two weeks after diagnosis, and was home from the hospital in an unheard-of five days and back to work teaching after only six weeks. Irwin had achieved these goals in part because it meant so much to him emotionally and psychologically to be able to return to the classroom, which motivated him to excel in facing his ordeal.

Irwin loved what he did for a living. He was a born teacher. He had been a teacher for forty-eight years. If you love what you do, you never work a day in your life. He loved the work, and it kept his mind off of cancer. He enjoyed working with the kids because they kept him young at heart. We both had been substitute teaching for the past twelve years in New York City. Everyone supported us at the school because we did it all and were very reliable. At the Gay Straight Alliance (GSA) yearly event, we were voted Best Student Allies and then won Cutest Couple. Last year's cutest couple winners just had a third child. Hope they didn't think that's possible with us. Our participation in school events and substituting was rewarding and fulfilling.

Finally after all the tests, hospital visits, and discussions with doctors, nurses, and support staff had been completed, the oral chemo drug, Xeloda, was delivered to our apartment, and Irwin began to take it on the morning of Sunday, May 12. I carefully noted this date in my journal. I wanted to document our journey as Irwin proceeded through the surgery and the drug protocol, recording the drugs' effects on Irwin. No matter the outcome, we wanted to preserve our experience for posterity.

Irwin was anxious to begin. He not only wanted to start the protocol, but also hoped to continue as much of his life routine as possible, which included continuing to teach and to share our lives with our children, grandkids, friends, and relatives. He had a positive attitude. He wanted a longer life so he and I, together, could watch our darling granddaughters, Maya, age eight, and Olive, age three, grow up. They loved us, and we loved them. Recently Olive had visited our apartment, and I said that we would walk to CVS across the street with Pop Pop. She asked, "Can he go outside now?" She was so happy that he could.

Maya had missed our visits to her in Philadelphia that before the illness were at least twice a month and every week in the summer. The last time we were there was the Monday before Irwin fainted at school. We didn't know what was ahead or how the protocol would affect him, but we hoped for the best.

Hope was the operative word. But we realized it could be months before Irwin was strong enough to make the trip.

The medical staff called Irwin Superman. He jokingly said, "I'll wear the cape, but not the tights." However, he was not comfortable with the label. He told me, "I am not really thrilled being called Superman. It's not about any strength, power, or perseverance that I might have, but simply that I don't want to die. I want to be able to teach and to be a part of the girls', the boys', and your lives. I just want to see the big beautiful tree that grows outside of our window continue to change its leaves and grow for many more seasons."

Irwin wasn't really Superman…he just wanted to live. However, there definitely were some inexplicable forces involved in his nature and the courage he showed.

6

FROM MANY MUCH WAS GIVEN

"People, tell me who your friends are, and I'll tell you who you are." I always said this to the kids at Delaware Valley High School-Student Education Center, which we owned and operated in Philadelphia for thirty years. The "bad" kids hung with the "bad" kids, the "druggies" with the "druggies." You get it. Now when I say this, I am reminded of the loving, caring, wonderful people who have been part of our lives.

We received a card the other day from Ela, Darren's friend for more than twenty years. We catered the food for Ela and Randall's wedding. The card was signed from Ela with a sweet message of love and support, and from Randall writing of how important we had been to them all of their lives. He also wrote that they hoped to get together sooner rather than later. Included was a signature from their daughter, India, and a drawing of a model T Ford and a note from Dashiell, their nine-year-old son, which told how he thought of Irwin at the New York Car Show because he knew that Irwin loved cars so much. He signed the note, "Your friend Dash." Something so simple and sweet, it brought tears to my eyes. Another friend, worried that we were working just because we needed the money, offered us a check anytime we needed it.

There are such good, sincere people in this world. Sam's mom sent loving, religious, and encouraging cards every week. Her prayer group at church, a dozen women, prayed for Irwin. Another friend, Linda, had her synagogue pray for him. Even our atheist son prayed. He didn't know to whom he was praying, but he was praying nevertheless. So many people called to offer support, and they told me that they were amazed by our attitude. They said, "Irwin and you are unique in the way you choose to handle this fight with courage and a positive spirit."

I didn't dwell on the negative or listen to unsupportive comments. I intended to save my strength and energy for the important battle ahead.

Now cancer was discussed or thought about in all of our conversations. Now our lives were different, altered forever and never to be the same. Irwin and I were beginning to change in our outlook about living and about what was important. Now little things that previously had aggravated or upset us didn't matter so much.

Because of his weight loss Irwin needed a new suit that fit. He wore his new suit to the awards ceremony at school and looked handsome. Then he said to me, "I don't want to be buried in this suit!" Cancer was always on his mind or in his thoughts. How could it not be? How could we not have changed, and not only changed, but also be different and better human beings? It was my nature to see the positive even in awful circumstances. But Irwin who always saw the negative was going through his own positive growth.

Our dear and wonderful friend Pauley recently sent me a very generous gift for her birthday. As part of her giving thanks, she wanted to acknowledge people who had mattered to her in her life. I was humbled by her generosity and realized that in this world there are more good people than not and that from many people much is given. I wouldn't allow negativity to take up one more minute of my time and interfere with our changing life. Irwin's and my metamorphosis had truly begun!

7

THE LUCK OF THE IRISH BECOMES THE LUCK OF THE JEWISH

When you are given a diagnosis of cancer, let alone pancreatic cancer, it changes your lives forever. Often Irwin woke up at 6:30 a.m., whether to go to school or not, and asked me a question about his doctors or meds or something related to the cancer; I knew that this question had been on his mind during the night. I couldn't have imagined how the idea of cancer would hound him 24-7. "Where did it come from? How long had it been growing inside me? Why me? Why me?" But then again, being the caregiver, cheerleader, partner, helper, and nurse, the questioning filled my thoughts as well 24-7! I don't know how anyone could do the cancer thing alone. There's so much to remember and do. I never had a phone call when cancer wasn't mentioned. Most people were caring and well-meaning, but sometimes it was all about them. One person compared his heart bypass as the worst surgery, and complained that his life was basically over because he couldn't be as active as he used to be. A friend said I was being naïve about the outcome. Another said that Irwin should be going to the gym to build his strength, as our friend did after his surgery, but I tried to let those kinds of comments roll off my back. People continually asked if Irwin had gained any weight back, as if this were in his control. It would be months before his digestive issues would calm down.

The day was May 12, and it had been three months since diagnosis. Our world had changed; it had been turned upside down. In the midst of this black cloud (*farsteranisht*, Yiddish for a life tornado), we smiled and laughed, and most days considered our good luck.

We were so lucky to be among the 20 percent of patients who were able to have the Whipple surgery, and that the cancerous tumor growth was in the head of the pancreas and not in the tail. We were lucky to have known the surgeon, whose expertise was the Whipple operation, and to have a surgery date within eighteen hours after diagnosis. We were lucky to have had clear margins, to go home in only five days after the operation, not the usual two weeks, and to return to work after six weeks. We were lucky to only have needed chemotherapy and not radiation, and to be cancer-free after the MRI's and PET scan results. We were lucky to have met Dr. Robert Fine at Columbia Presbyterian; to have had an amazing nurse, Dawn, to oversee Irwin's six-month chemo protocol and post-chemo care; and to have been accepted into Dr. Fine's important research clinical trial. So we looked at each other and, rather than being frustrated and fearful, said, "OK, we can do this." We hoped that the next six months would continue to be bashert. Lucky!

Irwin's plan to return to work in only six weeks was very unusual for this type of surgery. However he was very motivated because it helped him psychologically to not think about cancer every waking moment. Although he looked terrible, skinny and pale, it was important for him to do normal activities. He woke up, took his meds, shaved, took a shower, brushed his teeth, got dressed in nice clothes and hailed a taxi to school. He prepared lessons and was with the students who enjoyed his presence and his teaching.

Teachers would ask me if Irwin was all right. We never told them the extent of his illness, but just said that his kind of surgery required a year of slow recuperation, which they didn't question. He returned home by taxi, exhausted and needed a nap, however, he always looked forward to the next day.

8

CHEMO INFUSIONS BEGIN...OUR NEMESIS

Like anyone married or together for a long time, Irwin and I have had our ups and downs, disagreements, and differences, which at times seemed insurmountable. However, when we were faced with death, nothing else was important except surviving. This fight for life became our common goal, with each other and with our doctors, nurses, family, and friends. As we approached the next step, chemo, our relationship changed, and as our devotion and love for each other were tested, they proved to be stronger than ever.

The day was Sunday, May 12, 2013 (Mother's Day), day one of treatment. Irwin took 800 mgs of Xeloda, morning and evening. We were nervous and apprehensive. He had no reaction. We expected him to glow in the dark, to be sick, but he was normal (whatever that meant).

On day two Irwin took the same meds, and again there was no reaction. Irwin had an appointment with Dr. Haroutunian, the gastro doctor, who was pleased with Irwin's postsurgical progress. Irwin had gained ten pounds, had energy, and was healing and happy. He visited his periodontist Dr. Soman because for the six months of chemo, Irwin was not permitted to have any dental work. He was taking care of business.

Day three was the same as day two. On day four, at the hospital, he was to have the infusion for the first time. I was nervous. This was an unknown. I was at school in the morning and planned to meet Irwin at the hospital at 12:30. He was talking to Dr. Fine as I walked in. Dr. Fine was tall, kind, and soft-spoken. He really listened and was a little fascinated by our humor and by us. Irwin described the school we had owned in Philadelphia. Then he described the school where we were currently substituting, Columbia Prep, as, "everything you want and nothing you don't." Dr. Fine laughed. He explained to us that not everyone got all the possible side effects and was so cheerful and hopeful. We decided that Irwin wanted to be the best patient that Dr. Fine could have for this research trial. Irwin told Dr. Fine that he had been frightened by what he saw in the waiting room (old, sick, frail, wheelchair-bound patients) and that he was afraid he would be like them. Dawn and Dr. Fine explained that these patients were actively fighting cancers, while Irwin was cancer-free. Furthermore, each case was different.

The waiting room was difficult. It was where all the chemo patients met as they waited for their infusions and transfusions. Cancer knew no boundaries—it attacked all ages, young, old, black, white, Asian, Hispanic, rich and poor alike. The waiting room was a microcosm of all people from near and far away. As we waited to be taken in for the infusion of Gemzar and Taxotere, we spoke to others who were waiting; they gave advice and told Irwin that he looked great. They didn't know he hadn't had his first infusion. Everyone thanked God and said how lucky they were to live in New York City, which had so many excellent hospitals and good public transportation.

Irwin was finally called into the infusion center, had blood drawn, and got weighed, which was part of the routine so the nurses would know the amount of the chemo drugs to give him. Many pre-infusion meds, to help fight nausea, infection, and diarrhea, were administered, and then Irwin was hooked to an IV. If his veins held satisfactorily, he wouldn't need a port, a device that would be surgically placed under the skin in his chest to connect the veins directly to the IV through which the meds were administered. That decision was somewhere down the road. The infusion nurse, Monica, gave him the first drug, Gemzar. Luckily there was no negative reaction. This infusion took one hour. Then he was given Taxotere, the second chemo drug, for another hour. Again no reaction. Monica was impressed. Irwin had done well this first chemo visit. We survived the first infusion!

Irwin was hungry and wanted to have ribs for dinner. (Forget Weight Watchers for the moment!) Ribs! OK. When we finished at the hospital, we walked to a Dallas BBQ restaurant a few blocks away. It had a noisy, lively, fun atmosphere. How could we smile after what he'd endured? You learn that life belongs to the living, and we were going to be upbeat until we had a reason not to. This first chemo now in hindsight seemed like a piece of cake. Be assured that changes were coming!

After we had dinner, the A train took us to Columbus Circle in fifteen minutes. I picked up the anti-nausea drug prescribed by Dr. Fine, and we finally arrived home. I had left for school early that morning at 7:00 a.m., and it was now 8:30 p.m. It had been a long but good day. Irwin had a good night. So far, no side effects.

Irwin received a call from school early the next morning that they needed both of us for subbing. Dr. Fine had said that the day after the infusion, Irwin would feel strong because of the steroids that had been administered the day before. We went to school together. He was a little confused with all new meds he had to take in addition to the regular meds, but the important thing was that he felt normal.

We looked at each other every day and waited with anxious anticipation for a side effect. We knew that they would come because the side effects of chemo were cumulative. But for now everything was good.

9

DAWN AND US

I spoke too soon. Irwin had a little diarrhea and a slight sore throat for about twelve hours during the night. We were told to notify Dr. Fine about any changes so that he could document them as part of his trial. Irwin had a mix-up with the oral chemo, Xeloda. The next morning by mistake he took two 500 mgs when he should have taken a 500 mg and two 150 mg, for a total of 800 mg, but the doctor remedied this by adjusting his pills, when we went for the infusion on Thursday.

During May Irwin was in school teaching history. I tried to continue my life. After three full weeks at school, doing advanced placement testing and subbing, I shopped at the dollar store and Trader Joe's. VISA welcomed me back to the land of the spenders. We drove into Philadelphia with Olive, saw Maya play softball, and had a change of scenery. This was an exhausting day for Irwin (and me). I did all of the driving between New York City and Philadelphia and was happy I could do it. Although always interested in cars and one who enjoyed driving so much, Irwin was not able to do it physically or mentally.

Thursday, May 23, was the second infusion day. The A train took us to our destination, fifteen minutes door-to-door. Amazing—108 blocks in fifteen minutes. The public transportation system in New York City, and especially the subway, is incredible. First we registered with Kindra on the eighth floor, and then went to the fourteenth floor to have blood drawn. Irwin had to drink two quarts of Gatorade every day to keep his veins open and to keep him from being dehydrated, or else he would need to have a surgical procedure to have a port installed. We waited in the waiting room. Cancer knew no boundaries, and everyone had a story; however, all were hopeful. Cancer was the common denominator of life that brought people together as soldiers fighting a battle.

We waited an hour to see Dawn. She was wonderful, and we loved, cherished, and respected her. We brought Donna Bell's cakes from Darren's bake shop. She checked Irwin's vitals; took his temperature; weighed him; asked him questions regarding his taste, eyes, and mouth; looked at spots on his face; and reminded him to drink, drink, drink. She asked Irwin if he'd like to meet the man in the next cubicle.

His name was Jay, and he was in his early forties. He was handsome, with a beautiful wife and two young daughters. He called his wife, his saint. Jay had had a Whipple almost a year to the day before Irwin had his operation. Jay had never missed a day of work, had played golf every week, had six months of GXT (the same cocktail as Irwin), and came to see Dr. Fine and Dawn for follow-ups. He was so personable and upbeat. He was a survivor of pancreatic cancer. He told Irwin to listen to his body, to rest when he was tired, and to call him anytime. We all had tears in our eyes. We all wished one another good luck. This was what kept us going. We wanted to believe.

Sometime later that day, probably during the infusion, when all was quiet, Irwin said to me, "I can't believe Jay. He was only forty years old, big, brawny, with a lovely family, and I am sixty-eight. Jay was positive and strong in his determination after the Whipple surgery and six months of chemo, just like me. He gave me strength!" Irwin was believing.

10

SIDE EFFECTS FROM HELL BEGIN

One of my favorite movies has always been *Shawshank Redemption*.

I have watched it more than one hundred times. In a pivotal scene, Tim Robbins's character in the movie, Andy Dufresne, swam through three football fields in length of sewage pipe filled with waste and then crawled out, stood in the pouring rain, looked up to the heavens, and was victorious. Long story short: we were swimming through that sewer pipe full of shit and would be victorious at the end of this journey!

We waited one hour for blood to be drawn, so that the doctor would know how much chemo to infuse. Then we met with Dawn for an hour and then Dr. Fine for another hour. Then we waited two hours for the infusion to begin. The infusion process took an additional two hours. We brought a large bag of Donna Bell's for the IV nurses. Other than some burning in his veins, there didn't seem to be any problem. We'd been there for seven and a half hours, watched *Say Yes to the Dress* on TV (a mindless diversion), ate, and passed the time. It was almost like an indoor hospital-oriented picnic without the flies. We soon learned that this would be the pattern for the future.

We took the subway and arrived home as usual in fifteen minutes. We were finally home! A quick peanut butter and jelly sandwich, and both of us fell into bed exhausted.

Friday, Irwin was Superman. He talked a mile a minute and thought about cleaning windows and washing floors. I felt like I was hit by an eighteen-wheeler. The day after the infusion, Friday, it was expected that Irwin would "fly" from all of the medications he had been given the day before, but by Saturday, he would crash and feel much weaker. I did three loads of laundry, and I needed a nap. All I wanted was candy and cake. I thought sugar would give me the energy I needed to function. Yeah, right! I would have to eat the equivalent of a truckload of Hershey bars to give me the energy I needed.

It was Memorial Day weekend, cold and rainy, but the sun was shining for us. Irwin felt great, and we were grateful.

Oh well, in our hearts we knew this wouldn't last. On Sunday, Irwin woke with redness and swelling in his left arm at the site of the past Thursday's infusion. He had burning and pain, and now we had a problem. He also had rampant diarrhea. He took Imodium; the diarrhea stopped for a while, and then it returned with a vengeance. He was exhausted and weak; he had lost three of the ten pounds he had gained. Hard come and easy go! He was discouraged and disgusted. We left a message for Dawn on Sunday, but it was the Memorial Day weekend and no one got back to us. Irwin was drinking Gatorade and trying to gain back some of the weight he had lost by eating even though he was nauseous.

Dawn called Tuesday early in the morning and wanted to see Irwin immediately. Luckily a fifteen-minute ride on the A train brought us to the hospital. On the subway there were two elderly gray-haired women, who asked us how to get to Columbia Presbyterian Hospital. We said, "Follow us." A tall African American woman heard our conversation and wanted to join our parade to the hospital. One of the elderly women had heart problems. I described anyone older than we were as elderly, like we were young! The black woman had breast cancer, and Irwin told her that he had pancreatic cancer. Cancer was the great leveler, and we met its victims, of course, in the hospital, but also in the subway.

We arrived and saw Dawn. She looked at Irwin's arm and said that the IV needle had gone through the vein and had burned his flesh. Dawn recommended a port, which I didn't want for Irwin because I thought a port was a large thing with hanging cords and that required another surgical procedure. That was not the case. The port would be inserted under the skin in his chest. It would be an outpatient procedure, and he would be sedated. If he didn't have a port, Irwin would be at risk of his veins scarring and collapsing. Dawn scheduled the appointment for the port to be installed. We would try to get this complication under control before the next infusion that was two weeks away. Irwin was told to put compresses on his arm. This was all part of the process.

We took the A train home. Irwin was tired and suffered with nonstop diarrhea. This was one of the major side effects of chemo, and we would have to ride out his storm. He woke up every hour and took more Imodium.

11

LESSONS TO LEARN

I always write "we." We went to see the doctor. We went for the infusion. But in reality Irwin had cancer, not "we." Irwin had it in his head 24-7. Irwin had diarrhea and felt exhausted. He put on a good front, but today May 6, cancer had taken its toll—lack of sleep, a sore butt, and a salty taste constantly in his mouth. Then he broke down in front of me. This was the first time he had lost it (in front of me) since the diagnosis, and I started to sob, too. Recovery would be a long road filled with potholes. So together we cried. However, the tears were cathartic. The tears helped both of us and strengthened our resolve to continue forward, even when people had warned us to "beware of our bubble bursting and that things would get bad."

Irwin had always been a salt craver; now he only wanted sweets to neutralize the taste in his mouth. Yogurt, fruit, French toast—anything he craved he tried to eat. At times he put jelly and strawberry preserves on top of a slice of pizza so that he could sweeten the excessive salty taste.

It was Friday May 31, and Irwin woke up and felt good. So, we'd learned a lesson. He would feel like crap for three days, but then he could feel more normal. As chemo progressed, the side effects were cumulative, so the bounce back would not be as quick, but he would feel better.

One night, when his diarrhea was nonstop, I remembered that Dawn had said to use iron pills, which had the side effect of causing constipation and could help with the diarrhea. So at 10:00 p.m., I told Irwin that I was going across the street to CVS. He fought with me not to go, but I told him that I'd be back in ten minutes. I walked across the street and was back in eight minutes. We couldn't beat the convenience of a twenty-four-hour pharmacy just outside our door. The diarrhea stopped by 11:00 p.m. There were so many lessons to be learned.

We were both called into school for two classes. Irwin felt better, and everyone at school was happy to see him. This was so good for his head. Any diversion was cathartic. On Friday we drove to Point Pleasant and picked up Olive. This was our first time back to the Jersey Shore since Irwin's diagnosis. We had a safe and good trip. Olive grew more each time we saw her. She was amazing and uplifting for Irwin and me.

Irwin's chemo pills were delivered so that he could start the second three-week cycle, two weeks on chemo and one week off, so that his body could heal. If all went well, we'd try to drive to Philadelphia with Olive to visit Maya. Irwin did feel well enough to drive into Philadelphia on a Monday. Olive said, "Maya will be so excited to see me that she'll hug me and never let me go." We drove to our son's house so that Irwin could rest. I baked brownies with the girls, and then we went outside to play. Olive fell in a mudhole and came back screaming, covered in mud, but rebounded quickly with Maya's help. We went for pizza and ice cream, and sang "Happy Birthday" to Olive, who had turned four. Afterwards Maya gave her a bath, and we watched *Beverly Hills Chihuahua* and then had a sleepover. It was just like old times again. A wonderful, pre-cancer kind of day. We attended Maya's violin concert at school. She is a gifted girl, musically talented, an amazing student, and a loving, giving, and compassionate person. Irwin cried from happiness. When Olive saw Maya perform, she shouted her name out loud from a people-packed auditorium, and everyone laughed. We felt so blessed to have had this overnight getaway. We took nothing for granted.

We drove Olive back to Point Pleasant and saw an old friend for the first time since cancer had entered into our lives. He hesitantly and uncomfortably, embraced Irwin then backed off, saying, "Irwin, we don't want to lose you."

We now know that some people couldn't deal with cancer and stayed away for their own protection. I guess that's why there had been no contact for months. Perhaps this explained some people's behavior.

After we had dropped Olive off, Irwin and I had a lovely quiet lunch at the Shrimp Box, totally redone since Superstorm Sandy. The watermark in the restaurant was at five feet. We sat at the window, looked out at the calm water, and couldn't imagine what had taken place six months before because of Superstorm Sandy. Again, another ordinary, pre-cancer moment. We were truly grateful. We drove home smiling.

When we arrived home there was a message from Columbia Presbyterian Hospital that Irwin needed an EKG and blood work before the port would be inserted. The next day after school, we were at the hospital for four hours completing the pre-op procedures. It was a long day. We came home and ate a quick dinner. Irwin couldn't have anything to eat or drink after midnight since the port was being inserted the next day.

We set the alarm for 5:30 a.m. and fell asleep. The loud buzz woke us from a deep sleep. Once again, the wonderful A train. We arrived at the hospital at 6:30. The doctor met with us before the procedure and said that everything looked good. She'd let me know when I could see Irwin around ten thirty. So far, so good. I drank a cup of tea and wrote in my journal to pass the time. I visited Irwin in recovery after the port had been inserted. He felt fine, but there was a problem. The doctors had X-rayed his chest after the insertion as standard procedure, and they discovered that he had a pocket of oxygen between his lungs and chest wall as a result of the port insertion procedure. He had no symptoms, no shortness of breath, and no pain, but they wanted to keep Irwin overnight to watch him. There was a scheduled chemo treatment that afternoon that had to be canceled. We waited four hours for a room. Irwin sat in a wheelchair with oxygen in his nose. We had been up since 5:30 that morning and were exhausted, and I just wanted to cry from frustration. Why did it always have to be plan B?

Finally at 4:30 we were told that there was a room for Irwin. We walked to the nurses' station, and a nurse asked us if we were there to see a patient. It was surreal! They obviously didn't know who we were. We were taken to a room, which overlooked the Hudson River just south of the George Washington Bridge. The room was quiet and cool, and we were happy to be in a room. We were told that if the X-ray wasn't worse the next day, then Irwin could go home. I bought some dinner in the cafeteria and brought it back to the room. We had dinner together, and then I left to take the A train home. It was 6:00 p.m. Twelve fucking hours!

On Friday, I was back at the hospital. Irwin had had a good night, with no reaction to the punctured lung. That morning they took another X-ray, but we didn't have the results yet. Around eleven, I asked the nurse if she knew anything. She said the doctor would see us soon. We waited but the doctor never appeared. At 2:00 p.m. I asked the nurse again if she had an update and she said that the doctor had given permission for Irwin could go home, which was music to our ears!

We left the hospital around three o'clock in a rainstorm. It had rained every time we visited Columbia Presbyterian for procedures and infusions. Was there some hidden meaning in this? Irwin had been told to take it easy for the next few days. Everyone had said that a port was nothing. Nothing was ever nothing! Everything was always something! Another lesson learned!

12

A NEEDED RESPITE FOR ALL

Irwin returned the following Thursday for chemo. The nurses used the newly installed port to draw blood and for the infusion. This was much easier than being stuck with needles every time they needed access to a vein. We saw Dawn and told her of our mishaps. She said that we should have contacted her and was annoyed that the hospital hadn't told her about the collapsed lung. It seemed that one hand didn't know what the other one was doing. Irwin held his own—occasional diarrhea but controlled—and he was fatigued, so he rested. For this visit we had been in the hospital from 12:30 and finally left for home at 7:30 p.m. What could you do? The protocol was saving Irwin's life, and we were thrilled that he was part of Dr. Fine's group trials. The length of time spent was unimportant.

I was getting a much-needed break and was flying to Hollywood with Darren and Olive. The Los Angeles Zoo was honoring Pauley Perrette, the actress from NCIS, for her charity work with animals. She had been Darren's best friend for the past twenty years. She invited Darren, Olive, and me to be her guests, all expenses paid. I traveled light and brought only a carry-on. Olive was well behaved in the limo and was excited about the airplane ride. I discovered that the yogurt drink for Olive had opened in my handbag. I had a river of strawberry banana liquid in my wallet and all over my photo album. I borrowed a roll of paper towels from the limo driver and cleaned up the mess. After being given a diagnosis of pancreatic cancer and having suffered and survived so far, these small inconveniences seemed irrelevant.

I would be a passenger in Darren's car and be a part of his whirlwind life for four wonderful days. He knew his way around Los Angeles, so my brain was turned off and I didn't need a list of reminders. I was erasing my blackboard, which you should do occasionally to help survive your life. I planned to swim with Olive, look for celebrities, and relax for the first time in four months.

I walked with Olive to Hollywood Boulevard, a short distance from our hotel, and we saw the "real" Marilyn Monroe, Minnie Mouse, and Spider-Man, who, of course, were costumed performers. We had a wonderful time, and I was in my comfort zone, which had eluded me for months. Pauley's event was spectacular, with amazing food, animals you could actually pet, and movie stars casually walking around with their children. I met Katie, Pauley's publicist. Katie's mom had had stage 4 ovarian cancer and then had been treated with chemo and radiation twelve years earlier and was still alive taking care of her first grandchild, Mackenzie. God bless cancer survivors. I prayed that twelve years from now, I could tell people our success story.

Four days flew by in a flash—so much fun, relaxation, and enjoyment. Irwin missed me so much, but managed his meds, food, and well-being without "the wind beneath his wings" to help. This was his week with no chemo infusion or oral chemo meds, so it was easier for him to be alone. I arrived home, and we were excited to be together. Absence did make the heart grow fonder, even after all these years. It was a lovely feeling for both of us.

We drove to Philadelphia to pick up Maya and brought her back to New York City to see *Cinderella* and most importantly to be with Olive. This was to be Olive's first Broadway show, and she was enthralled. We were able to go backstage after the show and meet the "real" Cinderella. I took the girls on a double-decker sightseeing bus. We sat on the top outside in the sunshine. They were more interested in trying to touch the leaves from the trees that lined the sidewalks than in seeing the sights. Maya told Olive that the leaves were saying hello to them.

On Sunday June 16 for Father's Day, Darren, Olive, Irwin, and I met our son and Maya in Point Pleasant for dinner. Just like ordinary people. No talk of cancer. This was Irwin's off chemo week. He had less energy but wasn't too bad. He did feel stronger when he was on the oral chemo medicines, which was not the typical reaction. When we saw Dawn, she told us that another patient felt the same, which was unusual but good, and that different patients reacted differently than was expected.

Irwin started the pills on Monday and felt great. When we saw Dawn, she said that Irwin's positive attitude helped to make the difference in his condition. Who would have thought this about Irwin, who always had seen his cup half-empty rather than half-full and usually didn't have a positive attitude? We brought a large bag of Donna Bell's to share. Irwin had lost a little hair and was told that he might lose more. It looked like cotton balls, soft and baby-fine. Dawn said that his white hair could come back brown and curly. Life was full of surprises. The biggest surprise, however, continued to be Irwin's strength, thankfulness, and the positive way he dealt with his pain, discomfort, diarrhea, constipation, and problems of being a pancreatic cancer patient. We never realized or had even been aware of this part of his personality and nature... and more was to come.

Irwin and I talked about plans now with one-third of the treatments completed. Perhaps we would take the family to Mohonk Mountain House in the Catskill Mountains for a few days. Mohonk Mountain House had been a part of Irwin's life since he was eight years old, and we had continued to visit it as a family with the boys and grandchildren. We had shared wonderful times at this special place. It has been a hotel since 1869, and it was like staying overnight in a museum. It was set high in the mountains overlooking a forty-foot-deep glacial lake and was a haven from the problems of everyday life. The grounds and hiking trails were beautiful, the food exceptionally delicious, and the ambiance warm and friendly and caring. It had been a bandage on the wounds of our lives. We also thought about the possibility of taking a trip during the coming winter to Fort Lauderdale for a long weekend. All plans were discussed and then written in pencil with a large eraser.

We drove into New Jersey on Sunday to visit my sister Barbara, who was recuperating from rotator cuff surgery. Twenty minutes from her house, the power steering in our car broke. We managed to stop at the exit 7A rest stop on the New Jersey Turnpike and spoke to our son, who told us to buy power steering fluid. We poured it into the engine and tried to reach his house, which was forty-five minutes away. However, the fluid slowly dripped out. We were able to get to our son's house with not a minute to spare. He thought it was the clamp, but it was the hose that was the problem. So, plan B. We were getting used to plan B's—and plan C's. We took the car to the service station near his house and borrowed his car so that we could visit Barbara. What should have been a quick four-hour trip turned into a nine-hour diversion from cancer. You would think that with pancreatic cancer, you'd get a pass on the smaller stuff.

Ha!

13

PROTOCOL LIFE GOES ON…MANY UPS AND DOWNS

We were fried and exhausted and couldn't see straight, but we went back to Philadelphia on Monday to spend a night with Maya and Olive. Healthy people wouldn't or couldn't have done what we did! We had fun, ate, laughed, and enjoyed the girls. We returned Olive to Point Pleasant driving in a monsoon. No pass again. We arrived back to New York City at 10:00 p.m. and the next morning prepared for another visit to the hospital for an infusion. After what we had just put ourselves through, it seemed like relaxation time.

What I had noticed during those last few days was the way Irwin had handled all of the stress, tension, and pressure of the traveling and visiting family. Looking back, he seemed a little different. I always talked about "Pisces crisis" because Irwin would blow up over nothing. Now he was calmer than he would have been before his life-changing pancreatic cancer. Something seemed to be happening with his behavior, which was good. Hopefully the change wasn't temporary.

We arrived at Columbia Presbyterian at noon, an hour earlier than normal. It was July 3, and people were anticipating a long holiday weekend. A nurse hooked the needle into Irwin's port, and it hurt him. So much for the port being painless. The infusion finished at 6:30 p.m., but not before we learned that he had become anemic, a side effect of the chemo, and that he needed two pints of blood. His red cell count had dropped to seven. Anything below eight was a problem. We scheduled the blood transfusion for the following Thursday. We were told that if during the long weekend Irwin suddenly felt worse, then we were to go directly to an emergency room at the nearest hospital and have an immediate blood transfusion. This was like watching a ticking time bomb. On Saturday Irwin had a white coating on his tongue. Thrush! One more side effect added to his long list. Irwin seemed satisfactory, and at least we didn't have to visit an emergency room.

On Saturday, we were invited to a birthday party at the house of our friends, Gary and Scott, in New Hope, Pennsylvania. Irwin was not up to making the trip, so Darren, Olive, Sam, and I drove to the event. Our other son and Maya met us there. Both girls swam in the pool and had fun. About sixty people attended, which was a breeding ground for germs that Irwin didn't need or want; it was a good decision that he had made not to join us. Several people asked about Irwin. Some said they hadn't been in touch so as not to bother us, while others offered sweet help. The next day, when I called to thank our friends for the party, I was told that our friend, Scott had had a brain aneurysm and was airlifted to Jefferson Hospital in Philadelphia for immediate surgery. Man plans, and God laughs! One day you're fine; the next day you're in a helicopter en route to the hospital. The good news was that our friend was recuperating.

On Sunday Irwin had diarrhea and popped Imodium. Monday morning, I called Dawn, and she told us to come immediately to the hospital for the blood transfusion. We took a taxi to the hospital to begin the procedure.

Irwin needed two pints of blood, which took four hours to infuse. During the infusion he carried his IV pole with him as he ran to the toilet with diarrhea. We finished and were back home at 6:30 p.m. Another eight-hour day.

I ran to CVS before the pharmacy closed to buy the prescription-strength Lomotil for the diarrhea. I bumped into Olga Merediz, an actress and friend and neighbor of Darren's, whom we had known for years. She asked how Irwin was doing. I answered, "Great," and meant it. I told her that he had just been released from the hospital after a blood transfusion, was suffering with rampant diarrhea, and had lost three of the fifteen pounds he had gained. We both laughed at the irony of viewing Irwin as "doing great" even though he was plagued with so many side effects. We were beating pancreatic cancer!

I told Irwin this story when I arrived home with the medication, and we both had a laugh as Irwin ran back and forth to the bathroom. This ironic joke was not on us; we would continue to stay positive.

The diarrhea continued. Dawn doubled the dosage of the antidiarrheal prescription meds. Irwin was drinking Gatorade nonstop. He was told to stay out of the sun and out of the heat. Irwin was disgusted, having had diarrhea for six days, but his weight was finally holding at 116. So we said, "It could always be worse." He was told to avoid dairy, so I bought soy milk for him to have with his breakfast cereal. He craved chicken salad and macaroni salad (sort of an indoor picnic) for lunch. He felt like a prisoner attached to the toilet. We hoped that this would resolve itself sooner rather than later.

After six and a half days of diarrhea, it finally tapered down. We had learned that after awful days there could be a respite, and for that we were grateful. But Irwin's spirits were down as well as his weight. He had an appetite, but everything tasted like salty metal. He was sleeping often and long, which was a side effect from all his meds. He felt weak and had no strength or energy. It was ninety-three degrees, and we had to stay out of the heat and sun. We watched movies and tried to think happy thoughts. We hoped that better days were coming.

Irwin started the Xeloda the next day and then had the infusion on Thursday. There was a long heat wave of almost one hundred degrees every day, which was not good for chemo patients. We packed some sandwiches and Gatorade and took a taxi to the hospital. With chemo, which dehydrates the body, Irwin had to drink liquids and try to stay cool. The taxi cost twenty-five dollars, but it was worth it. Of course, all of the traffic was going in the other direction, and we wondered what it would cost to return home during rush hour.

We brought Donna Bell's for everyone. People at the hospital looked forward to seeing us and sharing our goodies. First they took Irwin's blood through the port. Then we visited Dawn and Dr. Fine. Irwin's blood results were good, and everyone was ecstatic. They told Irwin to continue to drink as much Gatorade as possible to prevent dehydration. We met with Dr. Fine's adorable son, who had just finished his freshman year at Berkeley.

During our visit, several other students and personnel also visited with us. We were their star pupils. Anna, Dawn's assistant, had been with us from the beginning. She had helped us with scheduling visits and test appointments, record keeping, and support and care. She did all of this with interest, concern, understanding, empathy, and humor. She laughed at all our jokes, even the off-color ones, and tried to understand our Yiddish idioms. She was our bridge over troubled waters.

We had a lovely visit and realized that Irwin's success would help to further prove Dr. Fine's chemo protocol was successful. We found out that Irwin's last chemo would be October 17. We were almost halfway there. We were thankful for a good week and a nice day at the hospital after many terrible days with bad side effects.

We had to change our plans that we had made for our Mohonk Mountain House family getaway. All plans had been marked in pencil and now had to be erased. Dr. Fine and staff were worried that it would be dangerous for Irwin to be around Maya, who then had sores in her mouth and on her fingers, which were diagnosed as a viral disease, called Coxsackie. This was so painful that she had to see her doctor three times in one week. We prayed that she would be better in a week. Again my optimistic nature just proves my naivety. We were able to switch the reservations until the following weekend, at a cost of $700 more because the cheaper rooms weren't available. I cried while on the phone with the reservationist.

I was at my breaking point. I was exhausted from eight hours at the hospital, with chemo, upset about Maya and her pain, and hoped that five adults could rearrange schedules for the next weekend. All of this, plus cancer and its treatment. Could anything ever be easy? Don't get me wrong; I was grateful every minute of every day for Irwin's opportunity to be cancer-free, but WTF! Our sons heard in my voice that I had been crying, and they told me not to get nuts and that we'd do what we could when we could. OK, I was back on track again.

Darren and Sam's cat, Sugar, went into a coma on Monday July 22. She was almost fifteen and was diabetic and received two insulin shots a day. Irwin and I walked with the boys to the vet across the street. The vet wanted to run tests. Sugar seemed to respond to the IV fluid that Dr. Walsh administered. We were so relieved, but he next day Sugar didn't eat or drink much, and we were afraid that she would die while we were at Mohonk with the family. Then miraculously she started to improve. The vet had literally brought Sugar back to life, and she seemed more like her old self.

July 25 was chemo day once again. It was cool outside, seventy degrees—a welcome change from the excessive heat wave. We spent the day at the hospital. We brought plenty of food and Gatorade. Irwin was dehydrated and needed a liter of fluid during the chemo process, which was infused through his port in addition to his meds. Dawn was happy with Irwin's progress, but was concerned about Irwin's contact with Maya. Coxsackie was not airborne, and I told Dawn that Irwin wouldn't hug or kiss her. Now our concern was Olive. Could the girls refrain from hugging, kissing, and almost swallowing each other with love, which were their natural instincts and behavior? It seemed impossible to think we should postpone this trip until the fall, when everyone would be back at work and school. More pressure. I didn't pack our clothes because I didn't want to jinx anything.

Life is uncertain, so eat dessert first. This had always been my mantra, especially now that Donna Bell's was nearby. We received a call from Maya's pediatrician, who told us that Maya now had whitlaw, a herpes virus, in addition to Coxsackie virus. Dr. Shapiro told us that because Irwin was on chemo, if he came in contact with this virus, it could be life-threatening. The day before, Dawn had also said that when she consulted an infectious disease doctor, he had said that it was dangerous and that Irwin should stay away from his grandchild. Ever the optimist, I had assumed Irwin wouldn't kiss or hug Maya, but "life-threatening" was another matter, and who in their right mind would take this chance? Sadly I called Mohonk and explained this situation, and they offered to refund all our money, even though their policy was to keep the full payment if we canceled within four days. They were incredibly wonderful about the problem.

I spoke to our sons and told them our decision. Before, I had had a mini breakdown about having to cancel the trip and deal with the disappointment. This time it was Irwin's turn. He said we should go without him. Not a chance! He blamed himself and his cancer. He slammed a few doors and then walked outside and sat in the garden in the shade under his favorite tree. I took half a Valium and then the second half, and then I took a nap, which helped me feel a little better.

Barbara called me and said that she was so upset for me that she pigged out on ice cream. Then Ronnie called and admitted that she, too, had pigged out on ice cream, topped with whipped cream. Then I got upset again. Irwin was still crazy. He refused to make any future plans that might have to be erased from the calendar and said that I should make plans without him. To explain his anger and frustration, he said that this was part of his inability to handle the cancer, chemo, and disappointment. We had a rough few days, psychologically, emotionally, and physically; it was a depressing time for all of us. These were the ups and downs of living with pancreatic cancer...but we were surviving. I was sad for Irwin because he felt so bad about everything. Of course, it was not his fault that Sugar got sick, that Maya had Coxsackie, and that our plans had to be changed. Mohonk Mountain House had been in New Paltz since 1869 and wasn't going anywhere. When the time was right, we would make this vacation happen.

I arranged to meet Maya and her dad on Monday July29 at Princeton Junction. I traveled on New Jersey Transit. Although I hadn't seen Maya since July in New Hope, Irwin hadn't seen her since our visit to Philadelphia in June. Irwin gave me explicit orders not to kiss her or hug her. I promised that I would listen to his instructions. Of course, the minute I saw her, I kissed and hugged her and held her little hands, sores and all. Then I washed my hands several times and used antiseptic on them. We shopped, bought Maya her school supplies, ate lunch at Cheesecake Factory, bought clothes for school, laughed, and had a lovely, happy time. Maya looked at the train schedule and begged me to catch the last train at 1:00 a.m. I was so blessed (even with the cancer swamp that we were living in) to have the special love of this amazing girl (and also to have Olive in our lives). This filled me up, and my cup overflowed with joy and happiness. The good times spent with the granddaughters always helped me put things into prospective. We had been handed a blow of epic proportions and we had been lucky, so far.

When I returned to New York City, I took off all of my clothes, threw them into the washer, jumped into the shower, and hopefully washed away any germs. I didn't want Irwin to be exposed to any dangers, so I scrubbed and scrubbed. I did it all for love, especially when my love, Irwin, had been given a life sentence of needed care.

I was the cheerleader and I would shake my pompoms when needed. Every day was an adventure, some better than others. I would not allow black clouds to rain on my parade. My visits with the girls would keep me sailing and feeling happy.

Since July 29 Irwin had had diarrhea for the last three days. He had lost weight again and was disgusted. This was his off week, no infusion or oral chemo, and he generally felt like shit again. We'd get through this, as we had in the past weeks. We took three steps forward and two steps back, but at least we were one step ahead. Ever the optimist! OK, here we go again.

The day was August 1 (August already!), only two and a half months to go. We had an appointment with Dr. Kadet, our internist, who literally had saved Irwin's life at the beginning, all those months ago, because of his no-nonsense, quick action and accurate diagnosis. He hadn't seen Irwin since February 13, when our nightmare began. Dr. Kadet was so impressed with his progress. Irwin gave him a brief summary of the past five and a half months. Dr. Kadet said that he had always known that Irwin had an amazing inner strength. Dr. Kadet said that he was not surprised, because he knew that we were smart, efficient, and thorough and that we got things done. Dr. Kadet hugged Irwin and wished him continued success. We were flying as we left the office.

Unfortunately Irwin couldn't seem to shake the blues. The effects of the chemo were cumulative. They became more and more potent as time went on. He was nauseous, so he took an anti-nausea pill as per Dawn's instructions. Dawn had told us at the beginning of treatment, "For every side effect, there is a medicine to help control it." Irwin had diarrhea, then constipation, and no appetite. This had been a pattern. We watched some movies, and I tried to be creative with meals. He loved strawberry jelly and put it on eggs, toast, and pizza. Irwin woke up on August 4 and pronounced, "I feel old, sick. Can't shit. I'm tired and weak!" And good morning to you, too! Sometimes it was hard for me, but generally I kept my mouth shut. He had enough on his plate, and his Superman cape seemed to be falling from his shoulders.

We planned to drive to Philadelphia the next day so that Maya and Olive could be together. They hadn't seen each other for a while. We had a plan. We would drive to Philadelphia with Olive, pick up Maya, and then do something fun. Irwin hadn't been to Philadelphia in six weeks. He hadn't slept away from home since the port had been inserted in May, when he was kept overnight in the hospital with the punctured lung.

This morning Irwin was anxious and had chemo brain, a side effect where the brain doesn't work as quickly and sharply for events and decision making. By mistake Irwin took both morning and evening Xeloda (oral chemo pills) at the same time. All of this was too much for him. He was agitated and confused and told me not to be angry with him. I talked to myself as I walked the six blocks to the parking garage to pick up our car. I always tried to give Irwin space when he needed it. As a caregiver I realized that I had to back off and not smother him with kindness, I needed to give Irwin some time by and for himself. However, at times I felt that I could be given a scholarship to a mental ward and a free straightjacket because of the pressure I was living with. I was not angry with him, but I was tired, frustrated, and always the cheerleader. I realized that Irwin needed space; however, sometimes it was overwhelming for me.

We drove to our son's with Olive. Watching Maya and Olive together lifted all of our spirits. They played bridal dress up and ate pizza and ice cream. The next day we planned a trip to Cabela's Sporting Goods near Reading, Pennsylvania. We drove in our son's new toy, an older Mercedes, and enjoyed the trip. At Cabela's there was an aquarium, dioramas with large stuffed animals, a shooting gallery (Maya is a marksman), a fudge shop, and a restaurant. We had so many photo opportunities, and no mention of the C-word was heard. Again the little girls were a fantastic diversion. We slept overnight at our son's and then returned Olive to her mom in Point Pleasant, New Jersey, and drove back to New York City.

We rested for the remainder of the day in preparation for the infusion coming again on Thursday. During our visit, Irwin told Dr. Fine and Dawn about his depression over the Mohonk family vacation having to be canceled. Our consultation group was growing. In addition to Dr. Fine and Dawn, there was Dr. Fine's son, still visiting home from finishing his first year at Berkeley, three fellows—Tony, Marnie, and Anna—and us. Irwin's fantastic attitude, which had surfaced once again from the depths of depression, and some Yiddish humor during the visit with Dr. Fine and Dawn seemed to lift everyone's spirits. The Donna Bell's pastries also helped. The visit was a shot in the arm for Irwin, who had been down in the dumps for days, and his positive attitude once again brought smiles to my face.

14

DON'T POSTPONE JOY

On August 3 we had dinner with Sue, one of our confidants at school and dearest friends. She had lost her closest friend to cancer in December and knew of the struggles firsthand. We enjoyed a wonderful dinner at La Mirabelle, one of our favorite restaurants. We spent three hours eating, laughing, and sharing stories. Her motto was, "Don't postpone joy." This became our anthem, too. We would face the future with thankfulness and with an upbeat attitude. We had come so far during the past six months and had changed in the process—especially Irwin, who increasingly looked at life in a more positive way. His glass was beginning to look half-full.

Sunday August 11 was Olive's baptism. We are Jewish but embraced this special moment because Sam, Darren's partner and Olive's Papa, had converted to Catholicism. Our family congregated at Saint Paul's magnificent church, across the street from our apartment. I believed that God had helped us through the last six months, and being in a house of God felt peaceful and calming. The deacon read some letters to God from children, and Irwin's eyes filled with tears. Darren prepared a whitefish salad, lox, and bagel brunch—very ecumenical. Olive was an angel, and her joy was spontaneous. It was lovely for the family to be together.

On Monday we met our son, Kelly (Maya's mom) and Maya in Point Pleasant. Maya and Olive played on a small beach, our favorite secluded spot. There were shade trees, picnic benches, close parking, a lifeguard, and a bathroom for Irwin. Then we walked on the boardwalk, and the girls went on rides and tried to win prizes in the arcade. We devoured a seafood dinner at the Shrimp Box restaurant and then had ice cream at Hoffman's, the best ice cream in town.

There was a sudden downpour, and the girls were dancing in the rain. Irwin was shouting at the girls, getting a little upset, insisting that they get under the awning, but they were having too much fun to think about not getting drenched. They stayed in the warm summer rain, and their shoes, clothes, and hair became soaked. At their young ages, they seemed to have learned not to postpone joy! For us life was full of impending storms, so we were learning how to dance in the rain! It had been a glorious day, and we felt alive and well—and there was no mention of cancer all day!

15

A BLUR OF GOOD DAYS AND BAD ONES CONTINUES

On a Tuesday near the end of summer, Irwin woke up and felt great. We had had a really good week. Most people took days like these for granted, but we didn't. We celebrated the good days, and when we had bad ones, we hoped and knew that these bad ones would come but also pass by.

Wednesday, August 14, was six months since Irwin was diagnosed with pancreatic cancer. It seemed like an eternity. Two more months of chemo, and then we would see what would happen next. This treatment was cumulative, and yet these past five days had been the best ones so far. Our spirits soared.

At the end of August, it had been two weeks since I had written in my journal. The week after the last chemo was typical: nausea, no appetite, diarrhea, muscle pain, and less and less feeling in his fingertips. Irwin was depressed because he knew what it had felt like to feel good, and he wanted more of it. We knew these bad days would pass, but it was increasingly difficult and Irwin was getting weaker. This caregiver sometimes felt the weight of the world on her shoulders (and I felt guilty for feeling overwhelmed at times), but I was not the one with cancer and Irwin was suffering.

We drove to Point Pleasant to pick up Olive. We met our son and Maya there and rented a speedboat for the day. Both girls were delighted and squealed each time we'd bounce over a wake from another boat. Irwin had a smile on his face (like a puppy with his head out of the car window) as the water splashed on us. He felt better that day, but we had to stop the car and then the boat several times to find a bathroom along the way. Superstorm Sandy had devastated the Jersey Shore, and it broke our hearts to see so much damage still in evidence nine months later. We were thrilled to have had this incredible day that we would long remember. Of course, we had a two-hour traffic delay at the Lincoln Tunnel on the way home. In hindsight it was a small price to pay for such an incredible day.

Sunday, August 25, was my sixty-eighth birthday. I was a drippy mess and very emotional—life and death are decided at the flip of a coin. I kept thinking of the one-inch difference in the cancer growth in Irwin's pancreas, but I kept these thoughts to myself. No negativity! We had a celebration dinner with Darren, Sam, and Olive. Irwin only felt fair, with no appetite. We ate cake (from Donna Bell's) and opened presents. We all made a wish and helped to blow out the candles. There was only one wish to make!

On Monday we drove to Philadelphia to have a second birthday dinner with our son and Maya. More presents and cake. More candles. Same wish. The girls played dress up and danced and sang to "Dancing Queen" and had a great time. We slept overnight at the house. This time Irwin was less anxious about the trip, and he slept well. We took the girls to play miniature golf, and Irwin was overcome with the heat almost to the point of heatstroke. He drank Gatorade and sat in our air-conditioned car. We drove back to the house, and Irwin chose to stay home, where it was air-conditioned, because he felt weak, while I took the girls to the mall, where they fought over French fries.

I felt fried myself and shouted at them to behave. They made up quickly and played at the arcade and rode the carousel. Back at the house, Olive needed a nap and gave me a hard time. My rubber band had been stretched to the breaking point. I screamed, "Fucking leave me alone!" I was, of course, sorry instantly, but it was out of my toilet mouth so quickly. Speaking of toilet, I clogged it with a huge wad of toilet paper, and then Olive pooped on top of it and Irwin had to plunge this mess before our son came home from work.

No, I'm not stressed!

And life didn't give me a pass just because there was a pancreatic cancer victim in the house.

We returned Olive to Point Pleasant and were home in New York City by 9:00 p.m. Thank God Irwin had the stamina to be Ethel to my *I Love Lucy* adventures. I took nothing for granted, and by the end of the day, thankfully we were back in our quiet apartment safe and sound.

During the last week of August, Irwin had meetings at school. He was so happy to be back, having had the summer to regain at least some of his strength. All of the teachers and administrators were thrilled to see him. August 28 was six months since surgery. Irwin was counting down six more chemo treatments. The next two weeks were a blur. Good days and bad. He was weak and short-tempered, and the diarrhea exhausted him. All of our plans were written in pencil. We managed to visit Philadelphia so that the girls could see each other before school started. This was my number two goal: to help my two granddaughters, each an only child, by nurturing the love that they had for each other as a constant in their lives. My number one goal was to keep Irwin alive and focused on beating this dreaded disease.

Irwin had two more infusions. His red blood count had dropped, and he would probably need another blood transfusion. We had a longer-than-normal delay while waiting to see Dawn. Then Dawn came to the waiting room and told us that she had a patient who wanted to drop out of the program with only two infusions remaining. Dawn asked if we would speak to her.

We agreed and met with this woman at the elevators. It was not easy. She was in her forties and wore a cap to cover her bald head. She showed us her hands. They looked as if they had gone through a shredder. This was a side effect of the chemo. She explained to us that she had had it! Her fingertips were so sore that she couldn't bear to touch anything. She was nauseous beyond belief, and she just wanted out. We begged her to try to hold on a little longer, another two weeks. If this trial treatment could ultimately work, she had to be strong and finish the protocol. Cancer couldn't win. Irwin, by comparison, looked like a he-man. We wished her the best of luck. We all had tears in our eyes. It was such a human moment. We were strangers crossing paths in this journey trying to help one another. Everyone's goal was to beat the disease, to survive, and to live a normal life once again.

I prayed that God would protect and guide us. I was not religious before our change-of-life drama. I had always believed in God, but not necessarily in church organizations. I had come to believe that someone or something had protected us so far, some "force" that was inexplicable but that was "there" nevertheless.

Irwin was awful the next few days. We knew that his blood count was low. Dawn told us it was 7.8. Below eight was a problem. We called Dawn on Sunday to try to arrange the blood transfusion for the next day. We spoke to Kindra, Dr. Fine's receptionist, and she arranged for Irwin to have blood drawn and typed for Irwin to be prepped on Monday and planned for the transfusion on Tuesday. We hopped on the A train and were back and forth in three hours. Irwin's numbers were so low that they arranged for the transfusion for very early in the morning the following day. Hopefully it would be the last one he would need. The previous one had kept him strong for quite a while. With only four chemo treatments left, we hoped this would be his last blood transfusion. We arrived for the transfusion, and all was good. No plan B needed this time, a pleasant surprise from our typical complications requiring a plan B and sometimes a plan C as well.

Summer was over, and both of us were back in school, which for Irwin had been a lifesaver in the past. It forced him not to think so much about cancer. He got dressed in nice clothes and did his magic with the students. He was a master teacher and brought the many subjects he taught to life. When teaching the fifth- and sixth-grade students, he often playacted scenes from different historical events with such realism that the students never forgot his classes.

Thursday, September 5, was Rosh Hashanah, the Jewish New Year, and people called to wish us a happy and healthy holiday. I was a drippy mess yet again.

I was crying and reliving the past seven months. How different could our situation have been? Our mantra was "four more chemos." We would do whatever we had to do, our exact words to the woman we spoke to at the elevators the other day at the hospital.

I had bronchitis and tried not to infect Irwin, who didn't have resistance to any infection. We taught school the following week on Wednesday and Thursday, two very long days. Someone asked me if Irwin was OK. We never discussed the real and true problem at school with the staff and teachers because we didn't want that *shiva* (Jewish for post-cemetery mourners) look. I replied that Irwin was doing as well as could be expected because it took a year for his kind of surgery to heal. Irwin looked thin and weak. Friday and Saturday were not good days. He was weak, tired, and irritable. I took walks to get away and to give him the space he needed. October 17, his last treatment, was thirty-three days away.

On Monday he started Xeloda, the oral chemo meds. For Irwin they acted like a vitamin, which was unusual, and he felt stronger and his appetite returned. He washed a window that had been repaired. I was thrilled to see that he felt better. We saw Olive, and she put on a show for us. She requested, "Ladies and gentlemen, please turn off your cell phones." She had three Broadway shows under her belt at the time, and she was an expert already at four years old. We had tickets for *Annie* for the following Sunday. We had made plans in pencil, of course. September 19, twenty-eight days and counting until the last chemo. We were praying for a return to normalcy in our lives once chemo was finished…"a dream devoutly to be wished."

We headed to the hospital for Irwin's chemo. After that treatment, only three remained. Irwin's legs were weak, but we managed on the A train. We had been warned that the subway was a breeding ground for germs, but it was so quick to get home and we washed our hands the second we arrived at our apartment. We discussed that he had three remaining infusions and less than a month to go and remembered when he had started chemo, five months before, and had seen people in wheelchairs, bald, and *farchrichen* (Yiddish for broken) and wondered then if that would be our future. Now Irwin looked like Superman in comparison. We were appreciative, positive, and thankful for every moment.

We waited an hour before his blood was drawn, and then another hour for our visit with Dawn. Waiting for Dawn, however long, was never a problem for us. In our anticipation of seeing her, visiting her, and being in her presence it was incredible, uplifting, supportive, and like a miracle every time. She is unique, extraordinary, honest, sincere, helpful, caring, and funny as hell. Irwin told me, "I love Dawn for who she is and what she does. She asks us questions, listens to our answers, and then asks more questions. Her beautiful blue eyes are the mirror of her soul, and they delve into our souls as she looks at and talks to us."

Dawn was astounded by how Irwin appeared. Several forty-year-olds were falling to the wayside and not doing well, and Irwin had surprised everyone. We brought Dawn lemon bars from Donna Bell's, Dawn's favorite. It was her birthday on September 19. The wife of Dr. Tony, one of Dr. Fine's fellows, was expecting twins on October 17 (the day of Irwin's last chemo). I told Irwin that I would buy yarn the next day and knit new sweaters for Dr. Tony's babies.

Because of all of the delays, chemo didn't start until 5:35 p.m., which meant we were at the hospital until close to eight o'clock. We had learned to be patient because we had no choice. Did Irwin want to see Maya and Olive grow up? We knew the answer and did what was expected. We arrived home at 8:30 and had dinner after a long but good day.

I was given a flu shot at school on October 7. Previously in my life, I would get white knuckles from my fear of shots and would nearly pass out when I needed one. Now I was calm. I told Lisa, the school nurse, that after cancer, ports, blood transfusions, and dealing with Irwin's surgery and post-operative care, my phobias were no longer a problem. Lisa, who had recommended Columbia Presbyterian to us at the beginning of our journey, and had assisted Irwin after he had passed out at school on February 12, asked how things were going.

I told her, "With Irwin, pancreatic cancer and 'lucky' can be used in the same sentence; we were lucky to have had the Whipple surgery and to have been accepted into Dr. Fine's protocol." Only she and Sue, dean of the middle school, and Margo, a dean in the high school, knew the whole truth about Irwin's condition. Irwin and I thanked Lisa the school nurse for her advice about going to Columbia Presbyterian. She and Stephanie, our son's girlfriend, were instrumental in our decision to choose Dr. Fine and Dawn.

Dr. Fine was in charge of trial programs for pancreatic cancer. He was the head of the Pancreatic Cancer Research Center—the head, not the tail (Irwin's tumor was in the head, not the tail—get it?). We thought the world of him and his group. We hoped that we would be a positive force in his trials and be one of his success stories. Dr. Fine and Dawn wanted us to be mentors for other pancreatic patients. Originally Irwin was too emotional to even think about it, but now that we were down to the last three treatments, we looked at this possible new phase in our lives with different eyes. Maybe we could make a difference in someone's life. I began to realize the importance of paying back in some way for this magnificent gift of time that we had been given.

Valerie Harper, the actress who played Rhoda on television, whom I've always identified with in wanting to be married and always being on a diet, had been diagnosed with a terminal brain cancer the previous winter and was given three months to live. That was more than six months earlier. There was a show with Meredith Vieira about Valerie and her cancer. She had chemo, and now in September, the doctors told her she was close to being in remission. Although she had already selected a cemetery plot and knew that she would not be cured, she had become a powerful example of what positive thinking could do. When she first went public with her story, Valerie said that she would think positive until there was a reason not to. She performed on the show *Dancing with the Stars* and she was living. Her doctors said that it was likely that she and her family could celebrate Christmas together. She told the public that she had hope and that sustained her.

I was reminded of that first night after Irwin had been diagnosed with pancreatic cancer. I cried and I prayed. "Please, God, give us hope." Now I thanked God for everything. The worst diagnosis, and more than seven months later, I felt that even with the pain, surgery, and chemotherapy, it had been a very difficult but positive life-changing experience. How lucky we had been. Pancreatic cancer and lucky in the same sentence!

We had a pleasant weekend with the granddaughters. Kelly brought Maya to New York City to see *Annie* with Olive and me. We ate at fun restaurants, and Irwin felt really good. We cherished these quiet moments of pure joy...and of living.

We experienced a strange euphoria. Perhaps knowing that the light was at the end of the tunnel had kept us grounded. We had heard a story about one of Darren's friends from high school, whose mother hadn't felt well after a day at the beach. She was diagnosed with late-stage pancreatic cancer and was dead within the month. How much did luck play in Irwin's situation? We didn't know, but we were beyond appreciative and thankful. We felt that "something," "some incredible force," "God" was working overtime for us.

Once we reached October, only two infusions remained. We saw Dawn, and she was amazed that Irwin's side effects seemed to have lessened. His fingertips were severely cracked, and Dawn gave him a cream that seemed to help. She had a good answer for everything. As usual, our love fest included much laughing with Dawn.

Our infusion started at 2:30 p.m., not the usual 4:30 p.m. We spoke to a man and his wife, who was one month behind Irwin. We discussed the protocol at Columbia Presbyterian and wished one another good luck. Irwin saw the woman from a few weeks before who wanted to drop out but didn't, and today was her last day. This woman and Irwin embraced each other and cried and hoped for the best. We and she were so elated that she was able to finish the final two weeks of her protocol. Dawn always reminded us that we might be able to help so many people as mentors. Of course, we wanted to give back and pay it forward, but we would have to wait and see.

The next week, without chemo, was thankfully uneventful. We lived our lives as best as we could. The off chemo week was generally not a feeling strong week for Irwin, which was unusual but time flew and he'd be back on chemo once again. Funny that he looked forward to being on chemo because he felt better.

We walked across the street from our apartment to shop at the pharmacy and saw an artist doing chalk drawings on the sidewalk. We were struck by what he had written. "You are an infinite possibility." We told him how meaningful his words were to us. He asked our names and put them in a heart next to the words he had written on the sidewalk. We took a picture of this and had it framed for Dr. Fine and Dawn. The words were clearly visible for more than a week on the sidewalk at this busy intersection in New York City. Another unbelievable, human, implausible story had occurred in this great city, where Irwin's life was being saved, and we looked upon the event as a positive omen.

16

IT ISN'T OVER TILL IT'S OVER

Irwin started his Xeloda and felt good. This was the eighth cycle—the last cycle. Five and a half months had passed—twenty-three and a half weeks, 165 days, 3,960 hours. And now it seemed to have flown by. Long days at times, dreadful diarrhea, constipation, destroyed hands, pain, and many other side effects, and yet in hindsight, we had come through it all, not easily but completely, and enhanced. He was a very different person, a new and improved Irwin. To paraphrase Thomas Edison, If you knew what you could do, you would be amazed, and we were amazed. Irwin asked, "Where the hell did I get all this strength"?

I answered, "It was there all the time; you just didn't need it."

Feeling positive, we booked a short trip to Ft. Lauderdale for January during winter break from school. An oceanfront room in a hotel on the beach would be just what the doctor ordered. We rented a convertible to prove to ourselves that we could do something normal. Could we think that far ahead? We could try! People were congratulating us already and wanted to plan celebrations with us. However, Irwin said, "No! I just want to get back to our regular life as much as possible. I just want quiet, rest, and to look out of the windows and enjoy the trees and flowers in the garden area of our apartment—and to live life."

We brought Donna Bell's and presents to the hospital staff for Irwin's next-to-last chemo visit. This would be his final meeting with Dr. Fine, Dawn, Anna, and the fellows who had become so important to us before we would start the next phase of our continued care. It was an important time. I crocheted matching pink baby sweaters for Dr. Tony's new twins. We wrote heartfelt letters of appreciation and thanks to Dr. Fine and Dawn. We gave each of them a picture of Irwin and me standing on the chalk art on the street corner and distributed letters of thanks to the doctor, Dawn, and the assistants.

I surprised Irwin with a gift of a Superman T-shirt. Dr. Fine was so intelligent. He exchanged quotes with Irwin from *A Tale of Two Cities*: "It is a far, far better thing I do than I have ever done. It is a far, far better place I go than I have ever known." Dr. Fine quoted Churchill, "This is not the end. This is not even the beginning of the end, but it is just the end of the beginning." Irwin and I realized that the first six months of Dr. Fine's brilliant protocol were finished and that this was "just the end of the beginning" because for a full year ahead and then for a long time into the future (God willing), we would be involved in more tests and continuous visits to the hospital with Dr. Fine and Dawn. We would continue to be a part of Dr. Fine's research trials, and that gave us a feeling of security, strength, and fortitude to face whatever the future would hold.

Irwin and Dr. Fine had an incredible camaraderie. I wanted to invite Dr. Fine and Dawn for dinner and to sit around like old friends (I felt like they were), but I agreed to put this off to the future. Dr. Fine suggested Celebrex as a follow-up medicine after chemo and told Irwin that he would be involved with his treatment for many years. We were a part of his story, and months ago I had written that we wanted to be successful for Dr. Fine's research as well as for Irwin's well-being. All of this talking delayed chemo until 5:30 p.m. It would be a long night. We didn't know how long or what would happen next.

It was the chemo infusion just before the very last one, but there would be some surprises. Monica, who had been our first-time chemo infusion nurse, couldn't believe how well Irwin looked and how fast six months had passed. She remembered how nervous Irwin had been that first time. It had always been like a freezing meat locker on the infusion floor. Even though he was wearing slacks, a long-sleeved shirt, a cotton sweater, a jacket, and my hat, Irwin was shivering out of control. He had always been physically warm, while I had always been very cold. I had a lower-than-normal body temperature and had Reynaud's, a circulatory problem that made my hands and feet numb. There had been a standing joke: Irwin opened the windows, I closed the windows, he opened the windows, and then I put on a hoodie. Now with chemo, his body chemistry had changed, and he was cold all of the time, which made me happy because he finally knew how I suffered.

At seven o'clock, one and a half hours into the chemo, the nurse took his temperature, which was too high. He was going into shock. Monica called Dawn and Dr. Fine. They prescribed IV Tylenol to bring down his 102-degree fever. Then they gave him a shot of Demerol to help control the shaking. The shot made him hallucinate. Dr. Fine and Dawn were now at his bedside constantly. Dr. Fine joked that Irwin didn't want the party to end and wanted to prolong his visit that day. They stopped the chemo and explained that he had gone into shock, which was a side effect of repetitive chemo infusions, and that they would get the problem under control. Then they suggested that we order a car service and take Irwin home. If his fever topped 103, I was to get him to the nearest hospital immediately! Hello, we're in a hospital!

We got a wheelchair and took him to an exit, where a limo was waiting. He could hardly stand up and was shaking uncontrollably. Even though it was about eighty degrees outside, I asked the driver to turn the heater on in the car. In the car Irwin talked like a crazy person, not making any sense. I called Darren at home and asked him to pick up the prescription of Cipro from the pharmacy that Dr. Fine had ordered and to meet us at our apartment building, because I anticipated needing help getting Irwin out of the car.

Irwin needed to be supported as he got out of the limo; we got him into the elevator and then to our apartment. He was delirious. His temperature was 102.9. Darren and I helped him into bed, and Irwin swallowed two Cipro. Darren left and walked to his apartment across the street. Thankfully his temperature started to drop, and he fell quietly to sleep. At 3:30 a.m. he woke up, we took his temperature, and it was 98.9. He took two Tylenol, and we went back to sleep.

Life can change on a dime. Many cancer patients often had this problem. We realized how lucky Irwin had been throughout this long process, even with a collapsed lung from the port insertion and all the other side effects. Seven days left, and we were counting. He rested the next few days, and we were grateful. What happened to Irwin was really serious and potentially life-threatening! Dawn told us this when we arrived at the hospital for the last infusion. Once again we were thankful, because it could have been far worse. Of course we were shocked but happy with the good outcome. Once again Dr. Fine, Dawn, and their incredible team had saved the day.

We had a busy week. We drove to Philadelphia for my fiftieth high school reunion. We saw Barbara and Fred, and then we drove back to New York City on Sunday and then back to Philadelphia on Monday to see Maya before Olive went to California for a month with her mom. We dropped Olive back in Point Pleasant, stopped at Hoffman's for an ice cream treat, and then drove back to New York City by nine thirty Monday night. We both taught school all day Tuesday. Did this sound like a schedule for two sixty-eight-year-olds, one of whom was on chemo? The next day we rested with smiling faces in anticipation of the last infusion. In hindsight, I don't know how we kept up this pace. We were running on adrenaline and nearing the finish line. (The finish of chemo and this grueling schedule.)

Irwin must have had a strong constitution to have tolerated the massive surgery and then the three-chemo cocktail during a six-month progressive, experimental chemo protocol. Recently, unfortunately, he hadn't moved his bowels for several days because of the side effects of the Demerol; however, he was always a trooper, but this time not a pooper!

We had heard from many friends wishing him luck on his last day of treatment. We were all smiles that day! What a milestone! People were so supportive. Greg, a pancreatic cancer patient whom we had spoken to many times during our visits to the infusion floor over these last few months, had been diagnosed the same day as Irwin, February 13, 2013. We exchanged e-mails and wished one another good luck. We had formed a bond that most people didn't achieve. With one another we shared a life-altering experience, and it was inexplicable and uplifting.

We brought enough cake from Donna Bell's to open a branch of the bake shop at Columbia Presbyterian. We saw Dawn, and she gave Irwin a framed diploma. On this diploma was written a dedication to his courage, strength, grace, growth, and complete metamorphosis under life-or-death circumstances. She said that she had only given one diploma before to a patient. Dawn said that she loved us and reminisced about Irwin's first visit with Dr. Fine: Irwin had been so tense and intense that both she and Irwin needed some Valium. Dawn told Irwin that his metamorphosis and his personality changes had helped him in his struggle. She was so proud of him. Anna, Dawn's assistant, gave Irwin a journal to write down his thoughts and feelings and a book about choosing gratitude. There wasn't a dry eye in the room.

We were given a schedule for the next year. Irwin would see Dr. Fine and Dawn every month for blood work and have his port flushed; he would also have an MRI and a PET scan every other month for a full year. We had been on a treadmill for the past nine months, including three infusion visits every month and many visits to the hospital, so this new schedule seemed like a vacation. We were grateful to be at this place in time. That morning I took a picture of Irwin in his Superman T-shirt to commemorate the day. He was just a little uncomfortable wearing it.

Now that chemo was finished, we were told that side effects would last for months. The next week on October 26 was our nephew Stuart's wedding in Philadelphia. It was an event everyone had looked forward to. We stayed at a luxurious hotel and could rest in between the activities. This was the first time that so many of the family and friends had seen Irwin since the initial diagnosis. Although Irwin was weak and tired, and couldn't eat much, we celebrated this happy occasion with a dance, as the family watched with tears in their eyes. Life belongs to the living.

17

SUPPORT AND ENCOURAGEMENT

Irwin was healing from the surgery and dealing with the many side effects of the chemo still in his system. It would take at least six to eight months from the end of the chemo protocol until its effects would completely dissipate. However, it felt so liberating not to have a chemo schedule to deal with. We remembered that very first visit and the fear we both felt about the unknown. Now, slowly, Irwin's taste buds were returning. He had a bite of a granola bar and declared that it was the best thing he had ever tasted.

Irwin was not a touchy-feely, share-your-feelings kind of man. He would never attend a club that he was invited to join. In a meeting with Dawn one day, she said that we would be great mentors for Columbia Presbyterian's Pancreatic Support Group. I immediately said that I would love the opportunity to give back and help caregivers, like myself, to better understand their role in this cancer process. Irwin said, "I'm not interested. It is too soon, and I'm really not strong enough emotionally to take on someone else's problems. It's not my thing."

Dawn said, "Give it time and see how you feel. It is important because no one knows what it is like unless they, God forbid, have to live through it." She continued, "You know the old saying, 'you don't know what it's like until you walk in another person's shoes.' You could be so helpful for outsiders, like caregivers, family, and friends, and it would be so important. I just know that you guys would be great! Let's just wait and see."

There was a Pancreatic Awareness Day scheduled for November 9 at the hospital, and we looked forward to attending. We listened to the amazing speakers (survivors), and there was not a dry eye in the room. We learned about the many advances and research that were being made in pancreatic cancer, such as the total removal of the pancreas and the placement of electrodes in a pancreatic tumor that couldn't be removed surgically but that could be electrocuted out. So many new discoveries were being made and new hope created. We were honored to be a part of this incredible program. We prayed that God would continue to bless the scientists who were on the cutting edge of developing new miracles. The fact that such progress was being made gave Irwin and me new faith, strength, and courage to face our future with pancreatic cancer. We realized that there were strong possibilities that Irwin's cancer could return in another part of his body and that continued research was so important.

Two weeks later Irwin was scheduled for a PET scan and MRI. We felt confident that all would be OK. Irwin was cancer-free when he was accepted into Dr. Fine's trial group, which included the six months of killer chemo (which killed everything, including his taste buds, appetite, hair growth, nails, and skin). Irwin was a big boy, and what previously had frightened the crap out of him, like being placed in the narrow tunnel of an MRI machine, now he took in his stride, even though he was still claustrophobic. Wasn't it amazing that pancreatic cancer had a positive effect on Irwin's nature and made him a stronger person?

One month after completion of chemo, we felt that we were home free and decided to try a support group meeting. Definitely a new Irwin! Perhaps? The Pancreatic Support Group Meeting was held on the third Tuesday of each month. This would be our first. When Dawn had mentioned this to us, Irwin was not interested in being involved. It was still too real and raw for him, and he was never a joiner. Although we felt the need to give back and would try to help people if we could, Irwin was still hesitant.

There were several people in the conference room, including John, one of the speakers from the awareness day. He was two years post-op. There was Carolyn, in the middle of her treatment, and her sister Nancy, her caregiver. There was a woman present whose husband, the patient, was unable to attend, and a young girl caregiver, whose mother was too ill to attend, but at the meeting, by way of Skype spoke to everyone. Finally, the three nurses who conducted the meeting sat calmly, smiling with twinkling eyes.

We all talked, shared, cried, laughed, and compared notes. At the meeting there was so much love and support. I was reminded of a lesson I had just taught the other day at school. The fifth-grade class had been reading *Walk Two Moons*, which I thought was about space exploration but instead was about a young Native American girl on a life journey, whose story had stayed with me. On the cover of the book were two moccasins, and now, as I sat in this small conference room, I fully understood what that school lesson was about. Walk a mile in my shoes because you don't know what someone goes through until you do. Dawn had said this to Irwin weeks before as she tried to motivate him to join the support group.

These good, kind people in this room had all worn moccasins on their journey, and we and their families and their friends were learning because, through these meetings, we were all being given the opportunity to walk in one another's shoes. This was a club no one wanted to join, but here we were. We were strange bedfellows, but all with the one common goal to survive pancreatic cancer. We hugged good-bye, wished one another well, and promised to see one another at the next meeting in a month. Irwin amazed himself and was wonderful!

A new spirit of joining in and opening up and sharing his life changing experiences was so fulfilling.

18

WHEN BAD TIMES COME

In the 1500s Shakespeare wrote, "When sorrows come, they come not in single file but in battalion." He had something to say about everything, and he was correct in this as well. Our battalion was upon us again.

We were back at the hospital to have Irwin's port flushed on Thursday, November 21, and to have blood drawn. We were anxious to learn the results of the previous week's very important scans. Irwin crossed his fingers, hands, and legs. He said, "I don't have a good feeling. I believe that if there was no problem, Dawn would have called us already." We said hello and hugged and kissed Dawn and played catch-up.

Dr. Fine walked into the room and said, "There may be a problem." There were several spots on Irwin's liver. I fought unsuccessfully to hold back my tears. Were we back to where we had started? Did this nightmare never end? Dr. Fine explained that the infection Irwin had had during the next-to-last chemo infusion, when he had a fever of 102.9 and needed Demerol, Cipro, and a limo ride home, may have settled in the liver.

I blurted out, "If Irwin was cancer-free in March, how could these spots mean the return of cancer?" Would this black cloud always block the sun?

Dr. Fine said, "The best-case scenario would be that this is an infection and that six weeks of IV antibiotics could fix it." But first Irwin needed a liver biopsy. I felt that the world was crashing around us again. Dawn said that she would try to arrange the biopsy for Monday or Tuesday of the next week, but with Thanksgiving on Thursday, who knew? Déjà vu, I had to call our sons, my sisters, and my sister-in-law with this new development.

I broke down, and Dawn said that she had screamed, "*Fuck, fuck, fuck,*" when she had first heard the results earlier in the day, and then she cried. She said she loved us, and then she shouted that she had to stop thinking with her heart and start thinking with her brain, which told her that cancer was smart but that Dr. Fine was smarter! Dr. Fine believed that the infection was the cause for the spots, but God forbid, if it was to be bad, then Dr. Fine would have a solution. We felt safe in the knowledge that there would be an answer. We had gotten this far and we would continue to think positive however difficult this was at times.

We took the A-train and headed home. I broke down a few times on the subway. We were blindsided again. How could cancer possibly have returned when Irwin felt so strong, good, and hungry all of the time? Irwin was expectedly stoically quiet, but I knew during the subway ride home what was on his mind.

The next day Friday November 22, my right foot had doubled in size. I couldn't put any weight on it, and the pain was severe. We were called into school that morning, and I hobbled along. I had a free class and was able to get an appointment to see the foot doctor. I hailed a taxi and was at the office in ten minutes. Dr. Dixon told me that I had gout and drew some blood to be sure. I was put on medication that would control the problem. It seemed that in helping Irwin improve his red cell count by eating liver, steak, and beef, I did myself a disservice by overloading on foods high in uric acid. I looked online and discovered that there were six pages of foods high in purines. Among that long list there were proteins, meats, shellfish, mushrooms, asparagus, broccoli, and spinach. There were four items that I could eat: low-fat dairy, multi-grains, nuts, and some veggies.

Wow!

We stayed in all weekend, and my foot started to improve slowly. Could it ever be simple? With all the issues we had faced, could we just have a little peace? "A dream devoutly to be wished," because no relief was to come.

We were called into school on Monday. We were hoping that the biopsy could be scheduled for that week, but unfortunately, since it was Thanksgiving week, we didn't hear anything until Friday, November 29. It was nine months since surgery. Irwin felt great and worked almost every day. His appetite was good, but cancer was always on our minds. The biopsy was finally scheduled for Thursday, December 5, at 8:00 a.m. Thank God Irwin had been called into school for photography teacher, whose wife was having their second baby. He was kept busy, which prevented him from thinking too much about the upcoming test.

When Irwin came home from school one day, he exclaimed, "I don't want to die." It never left his or my mind. We talked about the possibility that the cancer had returned. We both felt that Dr. Fine and Dawn had suspected when they told us about the spots on the liver that it was more than an infection and that the cancer had returned. I prayed for an infection with the possibility of IV antibiotics for six weeks. We hoped that if it was cancer, Dr. Fine would have options. Although we felt like we were back to square one, in reality the good news (always the optimist) was that Irwin was a superhero with the surgery and an excellent role model with the chemo. Now six weeks since chemo had been completed, he was stronger, his hair was thicker, and his weight was holding at 125, which was fifteen pounds higher than in February. I prayed that this nightmare would have a good ending.

On Saturday November 30, Maya and Kelly came to New York City to see the Rockettes. Along with Darren, Sam, and Olive, we braved the below-freezing temperatures, enjoyed a horse and carriage ride in Central Park, and ate dinner at El Quijote, one of our favorite restaurants. All normal fun things to do—the more normal, the better.

My sisters, sister-in-law, close friends, Sandy, Linda, Freda and the Bunishes called Wednesday night to wish Irwin well for the next day's biopsy. We all were emotional because the results of this test could change our lives.

We arrived by taxi at 8:00 a.m. at 51 W. Fifty-First Street, not our usual Columbia Presbyterian Hospital location on 168th Street. The facility was beautiful. The nurse took us to a prep room at 8:30. We talked about having to teach the next day and hoped that he would feel strong enough. The school was a great motivator; whatever helped us mentally was good. The nurse escorted Irwin into the operating room at 9:05 a.m., while I waited in the lobby, which gave me time to catch up on my journal. So much sitting and waiting and praying. At ten o'clock the nurse took me back to the recovery room. Of course nothing was nothing, and everything was something!

Irwin had needed sedation because the spot that was seen on the PET scan was in a difficult location to reach; however, he couldn't be sedated because he had to be able to cooperate during the procedure regarding his breathing. The doctors had told him that if he could withstand the pain and hold his breath upon request, not easy with his asthma and lying on his back, then he wouldn't have to return to the hospital and be completely sedated for a much more involved procedure. He did exactly as told, took no sedation, and held his breath as they stuck needles into his back and into his liver and completed the test successfully. He was starving when he was brought into recovery and ate a peanut butter and jelly sandwich that I had brought from home and half of my grilled cheese. He was told to have total rest for the next few days and he obeyed those orders by not going into school.

Superman could leap tall buildings in a single bound, and Irwin was leaping. He felt good and had a huge appetite. We were told that there wouldn't be any results for seven business days. We waited nervously. Dawn finally called us and said, "The three small spots were definitely benign, but the larger spot is still in question. More time is needed for further evaluation; I'll call you the minute I know anything else." She was our angel, and we were grateful for her beyond words.

So we played the waiting game. We were busy at school on Friday December 13th, a blessing to keep our minds occupied. When he returned home from school that afternoon, Irwin said, "If the cancer has returned, I will start chemo as soon as possible." It was on our minds every minute. How could it not be? Our future hung in the balance.

I was at school and called home three times to retrieve the messages. On December 11, after school I went to visit my ob-gyn for my yearly checkup. The doctor walked into the exam room and asked how everything was. I had not seen her since the previous October, long before Irwin's cancer diagnosis and the Whipple. I told her that Irwin had been diagnosed with pancreatic cancer ten months earlier. She turned pale and caught her breath as I quickly added that he'd had the Whipple surgery, had had six months of chemo, and was doing well except for a suspicious spot on his liver, and we were waiting for the results of the biopsy. Then I broke down and sobbed. The stress, pressure, and unknown results had made me a hot mess once again. She hugged me and begged me to call her when I knew something.

The next day, a week since the biopsy, our phone rang at 9:30 p.m. It was Dawn, and she asked to speak to Superman, who was sitting on the toilet, which he often did. I could tell by her voice that she had good news. The biopsy showed no sign of cancer. The spot might have been an infection or inflammation. She suggested another MRI in a month just to be sure. No antibiotics were needed. We thanked her and then fell into each other's arms and cried from relief and joy…once again we were so lucky and grateful.

We had planned a trip to Mohonk Mountain House with the family for the weekend of December 14. Now we would finally get away, celebrate the good news, and be "normal." Happiness had been a phone call. We swam in the indoor pool, ate, danced, ate some more, enjoyed the many fireplaces, ate some more, rested, and relaxed. This was a much-needed salve and happiness for our family. Although the temperature outside was seventeen degrees, it was warm and lovely inside this grand hotel and just what all of us needed.

On Tuesday, December 17, we attended the Pancreatic Support Group once again. We brought Donna Bell's treats for everyone. The nurses in charge, Marie and Anna Marie, and social worker

Geri, arranged a catered Italian Christmas dinner. So delicious! Door prizes were given to celebrate the holiday season. The nurses knew exactly what to do to lift everyone's spirits. They were wonderful.

We talked to the lovely sisters: Carolyn, who had one month remaining of chemo, and Nancy, her caregiver. The last time we saw them was November 19, when Irwin was scheduled for the MRI and PET scan. They hoped that all had gone well. So we told the story of the liver cancer scare. Carolyn had also been hospitalized for a complication but was recuperating. These conversations were par for the course, but everyone in the room knew what we each were experiencing. There was so much warmth and support. An attractive woman Martha and her daughter, Helen, had just received bad news that the mother's chemo wasn't working. Her doctors put Martha on a stronger chemo, which was making her terribly ill. She had been a smoker for thirty years. She was determined to stay positive and wanted to live. Another couple told their story. The husband had finished chemo three months earlier and looked healthy.

The group thought that Irwin was so funny and that he looked and acted a bit like Woody Allen. He was so open, motivated, and inspiring—I was in awe. This was the man who hadn't been interested in joining a group. Again the metamorphosis that helped him to grow and change continued. Everyone ate, laughed, and cried a little, too. These were real life stories.

We were proud to be a part of this amazing group. These people and the stories they related energized us and gave us strength. Dawn was so correct when she had suggested that we join the support group. She cunningly knew that Irwin would eventually participate. He told me and then later repeated his thoughts to Dawn that he had gone from "no" to "perhaps" and finally to a resounding need to become an active participant in the support group. Talk about change!

We were busy working every day at school. Irwin was teaching music and loved it. The kids at this school were so talented. The gym teacher needed surgery, so Irwin stepped up to the plate and taught gym to the fifth and sixth graders, a complete change of pace for him.

Winter break was soon upon us, and we eagerly appreciated the time off and looked forward to a much-needed rest. During the first weekend at home, Irwin said that he didn't feel well. He complained of pain on his left side and that his abdomen felt like it was on fire. Naturally he thought that cancer had returned. That nightmare was always our first thought. Would this dread always be with us? No major organs were on his left side, except for the kidney. The last MRI and biopsy showed he was cancer-free. This was a mystery, an enigma. There was no word on the next MRI schedule because of the holidays, so we waited.

We saw Olive in a Christmas Eve pageant at St. Paul's Catholic Church. She was supposed to be an angel, but they needed her to be a camel. She was the sweetest camel you'd ever seen. She smiled to the people sitting in the pews and waved and blew kisses to us. She captured all of our hearts. Then we ate a wonderful home-cooked dinner with Darren, Sam and Olive.

We walked home just across the street and prepared for bed. Irwin found a red angry rash on his left side, back, waist, and upper buttocks. The Internet (my other medical source besides Barbara) informed me that Irwin had shingles. The burning pain and rash were the proof. The pictures on the Internet matched Irwin's body. It was 10:00 p.m. Christmas Eve. I walked across the street to CVS and asked for calamine lotion. We were relieved that CVS was open. The lotion temporarily helped the pain somewhat.

Our plan was to visit one of those walk-in city MD offices, supposedly always open, but we didn't. Instead we called Dr. Fine at 8:00 a.m. at Columbia Presbyterian. Another doctor called us back and confirmed the diagnosis as shingles. This kind doctor called in a prescription of Valtrex. Irwin needed to be on this for several weeks. Ours was an ongoing saga. Irwin was uncomfortable, in pain, and very itchy, but at least it wasn't cancer, so we took it in our stride. We learned that shingles was another side effect of the chemo treatment.

We had planned a quick trip to Florida for four days in January to visit our aunt and cousins, to get away from the horrendous winter, and to just relax. I knew that it was wishful thinking to plan a trip—everything we did was always in pencil, so we could easily erase plans from our list and our lives. Just thinking about airport delays, getting to the airport, and the possibility of snow created more stress than a four-day getaway could relieve. I called the trip cancellation company and told them that we had to cancel our trip. Of course I informed them that Irwin had pancreatic cancer and was not up to traveling. They explained to me that the cancer was a preexisting condition that automatically canceled the trip insurance. However, because he developed shingles after we had purchased the insurance, they would be able to use the shingles as the reason to return our money. Isn't it crazy that having pancreatic cancer wasn't an excuse for the insurance company and that we needed another reason, in this case shingles, for the return of our money?

School was closed for the holidays, and we spent as much time as we could with Olive before she left for Costa Rica with her mom in January. Maya was in Hawaii with her mom visiting relatives. We had jet-setting granddaughters. We took Olive to the Big Apple Circus, and she squealed with delight at the acrobats. Irwin exclaimed, "This is living!" We tried to focus on the positive and not the new complication and discomfort of the remaining shingles.

Darren and Sam got married (legal in New York) on December 27, 2013, at City Hall in New York City. City Hall was like a sitcom in the making: men in wedding gowns; women in tuxedos; women eight months pregnant, here to get married for the first time as they held their young children in their arms; older men with younger women; and younger men with older women. It was a kaleidoscope of New York life. Olive was the flower girl, looking so beautiful in her fancy dress.

We grabbed our happiness where and when we could. We ate a celebratory lunch after the ceremony, received a parking ticket while we ate in the restaurant, and were very introspective. It had been ten and a half months dealing with pancreatic cancer, including surgery and six months of chemo. This had been the worst of times and yet the best of times. We hoped and prayed that 2014 would be a good, healthy, happy year. God had a plan, and we had a journey. If we had a crystal ball, would we have wanted to know what the New Year would hold?

I wondered to myself, *if we knew that there would be a negative outcome, would this hang over our heads like a guillotine and ruin any happy moments that the future might bring?*

Madison is our fourteen-year-old cat. Immediately after the New Year, he became very ill. He had always been challenged from the day we adopted him. He suffered with feline AIDS, digestive disorders, and diabetes and needed two shots of insulin every day. We visited the vet often during the twelve years since he had become a part of our family. He was an expensive pet and sometimes was ornery and aloof as cats could be.

During Irwin's surgery and convalescence, and during the chemo and recuperation, Madison's personality had changed. He became less independent and aloof and more loving, giving, and supportive. When guests came to visit, he no longer hissed and hid, but participated in the planned activities. When Irwin needed to be alone and closed the bedroom door, Madison no longer scratched or pushed the door open and didn't meow loudly. When the door was finally opened, Madison entered the bedroom and jumped in bed with Irwin, lay next to him, purred, and gently patted our superman's cheek with his paw. Madison knew and understood Irwin's condition and in his way had become Irwin's feline caregiver. This was so important to us and brought happiness and light to our often-dark days.

But on that Sunday morning, January 5, we found Madison lying motionless and having difficulty breathing. Irwin picked Madison up gently, but the cat didn't move or make a sound as his long legs hung limply. Frantically I tried to reach our vet and other vets in the neighborhood; however, none were open on Sunday.

There was an animal hospital nearby, only three blocks from our apartment. This facility was magnificent, beautiful, incredibly staffed, and unbelievably equipped. They saved our old friend's life after Madison had slipped into a diabetic coma. Two days and almost $2,000 later, Madison was back at home, walking more slowly, sleeping more deeply and more often, and needing help to jump from the floor to the bed. However, he was still with us. He had survived a life-threatening situation. Of course, he was not his old self and often cried after he had eaten or had used the litter box, but like Irwin, he wanted to live. Madison had become our "supercat." Our motto became, "The more we know some people, the more we love our pet."

As February approached we were reminded that the one-year anniversary was approaching. Irwin felt strong and had more energy. We were thankful. Dr. Fine sent us Irwin's schedule for 2014. There would be a doctor checkup every month at Columbia Presbyterian: his port would be flushed and blood work done. We had a standing MRI appointment for every other month, just to keep a watch on things.

On the one-year anniversary of diagnosis, we had our appointment at the hospital. On the fourteenth floor (the infusion department), we saw people who had played such an important part in Irwin's recovery. We hadn't seen them since October 17, Irwin's last chemo. They hugged us and couldn't believe how good he looked. We were so happy to see them. Everyone wished us continued success. After blood work we went to the eighth floor to see Dr. Fine and Dawn.

We saw Greg's brother and Greg's wife in the waiting room. We had seen this loving family many times during the past six months. Now we saw Greg sitting in a wheelchair. He had lost about twenty pounds and most of his hair. His coloring was gray, and he had dark circles under his eyes. He was unrecognizable from four months earlier. Greg spoke to us and said that he had had some stomach problems that he had ignored, and then he needed surgery. He hugged me and then Irwin and wouldn't let him go. It was as if Greg knew deep down of his fate, and this would be the last time we'd meet. We all promised to keep in touch, and then he and the family went in to see the doctor. Irwin and I cried for Greg. He looked like a dead man. Two weeks later, he would be gone. No one knew what was in store for any of us.

Then Anna Marie and Marie (wonderful caring nurses from the support group that met the third Tuesday of each month) visited us in the waiting room area. We hugged and then they told us that the woman on Skype at December's meeting hadn't survived. It was a difficult situation again for us. How were these extraordinary nurses able to handle these losses? Monica, another patient, who had lost all of her hair, and her husband were introduced to us. She was Dr. Fine's patient. She was about forty and had been diagnosed two and a half years earlier, given six months to live, and was still here bravely fighting her battle. She said that she would see us at the support meeting the following Tuesday.

Finally Dr. Fine called us into the office. We told him that we missed him, Dawn, and his staff so much. They had been and would be a part of our lives forever. We expressed our feelings regarding Greg and that both of us were very upset by Greg's appearance.

Then we discussed Irwin's emotional feelings of sadness and sorrow and fear with Dawn. Irwin asked, "How do you handle the overwhelming loss of patients and people you have been treating?"

Dawn answered, "I have to remain strong and think about what I was able to do while the person was alive. I try to move forward and pick up the pieces of my sad heart, which isn't easy." Dawn added, "You and Audrey should try not to internalize the sadness, if you can, and don't be afraid. Cancer is smart, but Dr. Fine is smarter."

19

SHARED MOMENTS AND PERSONAL GROWTH

There was chemistry among Dawn, Irwin, and me. We "got" one another. Dawn knew something about everything, and she understood people. She was brilliant, sensitive, and very funny. We told her that we had had successful sex the other day and that unexpectedly things were OK. At that important moment, Irwin had said, "Wait until I tell Dawn." Incredibly in the middle of it all, Irwin thought about Dawn. We howled with laughter, and then Dawn said, "This is really sick," and then we laughed some more. We were attached at the hip, till death do us part.

Dr. Fine, who may be the smartest doctor on the planet, said in Greek, "The die is cast," words from Shakespeare's Julius Caesar. Irwin replied, "You are my captain, and I will follow you anywhere." This was a moment in time not to be forgotten. Irwin told Dr. Fine that today was his one-year anniversary since being diagnosed. He was so happy and animated that Dr. Fine wanted to know if Irwin could get for him whatever it was that Irwin had smoked. Again everyone howled with laughter. We were on an emotional rollercoaster. We cried one minute and laughed the next. The tears were tears of happiness.

We spoke about the recent death of the great actor Philip Seymour Hoffman. We had known him personally through Darren. We attended parties with him and his wife, Mimi; they were such warm people. Phil was in rehab twenty-five years earlier and recently had relapsed to using heroin again. Irwin was adamant about not feeling sorry for the actor, who had talent, fame, money, and a loving family. Irwin said, "When Audrey and I sit in a room on the fourteenth floor as we wait for chemo and watch people who have endured indignities, pain and suffering, sadness, humiliation, alienation, and despair and see how they fight like hell to live; and here is this famous, gifted actor who overdosed on heroin, I can't feel sympathy."

Dawn said to Irwin, "You should be more understanding in your opinion because Hoffman's drug addiction was a disease, and just like any other disease, he had gone through his own hell." She always seemed to have the right answer!

How had Irwin become Superman? Did his will to live overpower the cancer? I saw Emme, the first "large" fashion supermodel, a five-year survivor of cancer, on TV. She said, "I believe that God is using me to help get the message across that you must be your own advocate to overpower cancer. You must listen to your body and find the best medical care, which sometimes is pure luck." This supermodel became her own "superwoman." We had been lucky in so many ways, and especially in the strength that Irwin, our own "superman," had shown all during his journey.

Since the December support meeting, I had been mentoring Martha, a lovely woman in her midfifties, who was unable to have the Whipple surgery, and for whom, so far, chemo had not been successful. Now she was having radiation for six weeks. When I spoke to her over the phone, she wanted to know if I knew anyone who could help her. She was a retired airline employee, who needed to supplement her income, and wanted to clean houses, but was too weak. I admired her spirit and courage. Martha lived with her daughter, Helen, whose small salary was still too much for Martha to qualify for financial aid. I was outraged. The injustice made me so angry. I asked the nurses from the support group if there was any help for Martha, and they shook their heads no. Doctors who saved lives had to beg for donations to help continue pancreatic cancer research, as did Dr. Fine. Why wasn't the public more interested in helping fight one of the worst cancers? Celebrities Patrick Swayze, Bonnie Franklin, Pavarotti, Steve Jobs and Katie Couric's sister all had died from this killer. People were dying every day. Where was the outcry to try to find procedures for early detection, which was so important?

We met with the support group on the third Tuesday of each month. There was no meeting in January because of the foul weather. Now only three patients and their caregivers attended. At the February meeting, Irwin celebrated his one-year anniversary since diagnosis. Carolyn had finished her six months of chemo and had her port removed. Geri, the group counselor, conducted the meeting and asked how everyone's holidays had been. Monica had had a house fire on January 9, and her four-year-old was living with relatives out of state because of the damage. She was fighting with her landlord and the insurance company to get the repairs finished; there was so much red tape and never-ending problems and delays. Carolyn and her sister Nancy had helped their elderly parents pack up their family home and move to an assisted living facility. No one was given a free pass from problems that came with living life just because they suffered with pancreatic cancer. During the meeting it seemed to comfort all of us as we shared our experiences; this gave us strength. All of us, and especially the caregivers, were walking in one another's shoes.

After the meeting Irwin and I had dinner at the Reme diner near the hospital. We had eaten there a few times, the food was good and reasonably priced, but we felt very different now—and happier since Irwin's chemo protocol treatment had been completed. Our lives continued as Irwin felt stronger and had gained a few more pounds. Wow, 128 pounds!

A college friend of Darren's, whose father had been a general in the army, had been diagnosed with pancreatic cancer about the same time as Irwin. We had spent a wonderful Christmas at their home in Hilton Head more than twenty years earlier. Her dad was a big, strong, strapping man, and he had passed away within six months from pancreatic cancer. A good man had gone too soon. The many people who we had heard hadn't survived made us even more determined to live our lives as well as we could and to believe and to fight on.

Early in March we ordered tickets to see an off-Broadway show, our first since treatment finished. After all of the bad winter weather, this was a glorious day. The temperature unexpectedly approached sixty degrees, the sun shone brightly, and we walked in Union Square, sat on a park bench, and watched the people pass by. The show, *Till Divorce Do Us Part*, was funny and clever. A teacher, John Fischer, from our school had written the music, and we were glad to support his efforts.

We walked across the park after the show and went to the Coffee Shop, an old favorite of ours. We hadn't been there since we had moved to New York fourteen years earlier. All of the staff were beautiful actors and actresses who had kept their day jobs while they waited for their lucky breaks in show business. We had so many fond memories of the meals we had shared with Darren and his many friends. As we sat at our table, Irwin broke down and started to cry. He was very emotional these days, having survived his ordeal. He asked the waiter for more napkins to wipe away his tears. These were not tears of sadness, but tears of gratitude and joy. He was grateful and happy to have seen a show and to have eaten a delicious meal just like other people. It was a lovely date night and a return to normalcy. We were so thankful.

I moved the clocks ahead for daylight saving time. Spring ahead, fall back, and we were springing ahead in many ways. I woke up unusually early because of the time change. I walked into the living room and turned on the TV, which had become my favorite sleeping aid. I often did this to help take my mind off of the many thoughts swirling in my head. I normally only needed a few "bebumps" to fall to sleep again. That morning as I watched a Law and Order episode I was drawn into the story. Lt. VanBuren was having an MRI. She had been treated for cancer in a previous story line. This episode required her to have another MRI because the results were unclear. In a very dramatic ending, Lt. VanBuren received a call from her doctor. The viewer only saw her back. I watched her shoulders drop as her body shook. The viewer, of course, assumed the worst. Then the camera showed her face as she looked up to the heavens and mouthed the words, "Thank you, God" as tears streamed down her face. There were tears streaming down my face also, as I said, "Thank you, God." Cancer was all around us, every day, for thousands of people.

March 12 was Irwin's sixty-ninth birthday. It had been thirteen months since diagnosis, and our journey continued. (I had thought that this would be the ending to my book.) Dawn, our nurse (goddess), and Anna (our angel) called and asked to speak to Superman. Irwin picked up the phone, and they sang "Happy Birthday" to him. In our or your entire lives, did we ever hear of a doctor's office that called to sing "Happy Birthday"? Columbia Presbyterian Hospital was an unbelievable, incredible, uncommon, one-of-a-kind hospital (OK, you get it)! We loved its staff and our doctors and nurses and everything they did. They were saving lives! This birthday was a reality check. Irwin was still here, and we were returning to normal. Every day was a gift, and we knew it. There was not a moment that we were not grateful and motivated about the future, even as we faced potential problems. From dark clouds we saw beautiful rainbows.

We attended the March support group meeting. Several new people with the dreaded disease were present. A sixty-two-year-old woman from New Jersey had been told that she had inoperable stage 4 pancreatic cancer, and the woman's daughter and a friend were at the meeting with her. On January 1 her world collapsed when she was told of her illness. As we sat around the table, everyone offered her advice and support. A man from Long Island, in his sixties, had had the Whipple in November and was having chemo at Memorial Sloan Kettering. He had come to Columbia Presbyterian for the support group because Columbia Presbyterian Hospital was the only one that offered a pancreatic cancer support group in the entire area. We were all in the same cancer boat, hopeful, helpful, and frightened for one another and ourselves. This meeting, as all the others, was humbling, exhilarating, sad, happy, difficult, poignant, heartbreaking, strengthening—and necessary.

There were only a few people present at the April meeting because it was Passover. I brought Donna Bell's treats, and everyone ate something good. A cupcake could help to make your day! There had been a man in the waiting room who we recognized from the Pancreas Awareness Day last November. John was from England and had had the Whipple three years earlier. He told us that he had been experiencing some stomach discomfort during the last few months. This morning he had his last protocol-scheduled MRI (every three months for two years), and the doctors saw something suspicious. Hopefully it would only be an infection (please, God), but he needed a PET scan the next day to find out. Then he started to cry and hugged Irwin so tightly that he couldn't breathe. Irwin and I started to cry, too, because this nightmare was always lurking in the shadows, waiting, waiting for all of us because even with a Whipple surgery, the percentage of cancer returning somewhere else in your body was very high. We told John that if cancer had returned, God forbid, it hadn't been there three months earlier when he had had his last MRI and that it would be an early stage in a new location. We wished him good luck, and we all hugged again. Remember, Irwin had never been a hugger before.

At the meeting we all sat around and talked about our situations. Martha had encouraging news. Her tumor had shrunk by half. I'd spoken to her over the last several months, and she called me her angel, her sister. Martha's tumor was inoperable and it had not responded to the first chemo protocol, but the current radiation had done its job and had reduced the tumor by half. However, she said, "Radiation was unbearable. I was nauseous, vomited, and suffered with nonstop impossible heartburn, which kept me up at night." She had thirty rounds of radiation, but physically had to stop.

She went back to her native country, Santo Domingo, for a much-needed rest. She lived with Helen, her daughter, who was her caregiver. Although English was her second language, she was well-spoken. Her doctors wanted her to begin a new and different round of chemo, which she gladly accepted. She wanted to live and wanted to have hope. She said people were kind but didn't fully understand the scope and nature of this horrendous disease. She said that some of her family and friends ignored her and kept their distance because they assumed that she was dying and wanted to avoid seeing her up close. (We had experienced similar behavior.) Martha said the support group had given her courage, and everyone agreed. The nurses explained that they gave everyone as much love, respect, and care as they could.

We were grateful that Columbia Presbyterian had a support group with such wonderful nurses, who helped so much, because it was so needed. We were like a family, who listened to one another. We all wanted good outcomes and hoped that pancreatic cancer researchers would find the answers in the battle against the disease. However, for this to happen, much money would be needed. Irwin and I have decided that we will share the proceeds of this book with Dr. Fine's research group. We learned of the need and we have been given so much, we will give back when and how we can. God had been good to us and we would never forget it.

20

A METAMORPHOSIS AND A GIFT

Recently I read about something called posttraumatic growth in the AARP magazine. This is something that occurs in people's personalities after experiencing life-altering, life-changing events. A man who survived the airplane landing in the Hudson River gave up the job he'd cared about and went on to work with seniors and was inspired to write a book about his experiences. Irwin and I now felt that there was a calling for us, not to just go through life as in a dream, but to step up and live every minute to the fullest, because time is a rare, priceless, and wonderful gift. We had learned that the purpose of our lives now would include a bigger picture and that, hopefully, we had become kinder, wiser, gentler people. Irwin, who needed personal psychological change in his life, had experienced a metamorphosis during this past year, and a new way of living increased our hope.

This is not the beginning of our story, nor is it the end; rather, it is just the end of the beginning. Our story is not complete, but it is a moment, a defining glimpse, in time. We will continue to move forward on the train of time (our A subway) as we proceed on our journey. We will live with pancreatic cancer issues. Irwin will take his four shots of insulin a day, prick his fingertips three times a day to evaluate his glucose levels, and swallow his handful of eighteen pills a day. He will follow Dr. Fine's ongoing post-chemo protocol for a very long time, and we will be avid support group participants. I will continue to be the "wind beneath his wings" (as he describes me), and we will not just wait for the impending storm but continue to learn how to dance new dances in the rain…and amaze ourselves in the process.

Our story has been personal, telling how our lives changed on February 13, 2013, at 5:00 p.m. I wrote this book to document our journey and to explain the good and the bad, the joy and the sadness, and the rejuvenation after the heartache. For Irwin and me, our two sons, son-in-law, granddaughters and our family and friends, it was the worst of times and also the best of times.

Dawn called the other night. I answered the phone, and after asking how she was, I told her that I would put Irwin on the phone.

She said, "I want to speak to you, and I need a favor."

I replied, "Anything." I didn't need to think twice because I love Dawn and her team and would do anything she asked. She had been responsible for prolonging Irwin's life and helping him through the darkest of days.

Dawn said, "Please call the wife of a man dying from pancreatic cancer. She is in total denial of this grave situation." Dawn trusted and believed that I had become a unique caregiver, because I knew when to back off and give Irwin time and space to deal with his illness.

I called the woman, and we spoke for two hours. She explained that she and her husband were in their early fifties, had grown children, enjoyed a lovely privileged life including hobbies and vacations, and had so much to look forward to. Although we were in our late sixties, it was not unlike the life we had lived. We shared stories about our lives and families. She said, "Pancreatic cancer isn't fair."

I replied, "So much of life isn't fair—the shootings at Newtown, the Boston Marathon terrorists, and 9/11, for example." I continued, "On the mornings of those horrific events, did anyone know that their loved ones would be gone? Don't waste one moment while your husband is alive; help him find peace knowing that you and your family will be all right." I added, "You and your husband must cherish every second, resolve any issues, and leave nothing unsaid. This would be a gift for him, and if you have to hide in the shower and sob, so be it."

We agreed to keep in touch. Irwin had had his metamorphosis, and I had been given a gift. I realize now that I have an ability to help others and that I need to give back because of the amazing gift of time that Irwin and I have been given. Our love, strength, and survival with this dreaded disease was one in a million. Because of the support group, there would be people who could benefit from our positive experience. Pancreatic cancer and lucky could be said in the same sentence. We have learned that cancer can be a wake-up call. You must live your life as if each day were your last; don't waste a minute. Find meaning in what you do and enjoy your life because no one knows the time any of us has. Learn to turn a problem into an opportunity for personal growth and development. Make the best of any situation because you have the choice to do so.

21

EPILOGUE

As I finish writing this book, it is now twenty months since diagnosis. It has been interesting because on any given day, I could tell you how many months and weeks it was since we were told that Irwin had pancreatic cancer. Time never mattered so much before, but now the gift of time that we have been given has meant so much to us. We have been changed forever by events and have learned about a better, kinder, gentler way to live. We are thankful for our changed life every day. That dramatic fateful day, February 13, 2013, was one we will never forget. Pancreatic cancer has become the framework of our lives. It is the common denominator that has influenced who we are, what we have become, and who we will be in the future—and we are happy.

We had to put our beloved cat Madison to sleep. He had been given a gift since last January, when he went into a diabetic coma. For these last nine months, he continued to lose weight and had cancer and heart disease. He had been a member of our family and Irwin's feline caregiver, and he will be greatly missed. Irwin has been having a difficult time with his loss, but life continues. He waits for the change from sadness to sweet memories, when he will look at pictures of Madison and finally they will bring him comfort and happiness.

Monday we hopped the A train to the hospital. I looked at the people's faces on the subway and made up scenarios about their lives as I often did. I asked myself, were they healthy? What problems plagued them? Were they happy? What stress did they live with? Were they thankful about their lives? This reinforced my own feelings about my life because I realized how lucky we had been on our journey.

During the hospital visit Monday, Irwin was given his semi-monthly blood work and scheduled MRIs of his pelvis and abdomen with and without contrast and a chest CT scan, all starting at noon. Previously this would have struck fear in his heart, and he would have needed a Valium drip. Now he took all of this in stride and hoped for a good outcome.

Irwin couldn't eat anything past 11:00 a.m. Unfortunately, there were several delays, and the final MRI didn't start until 6:00 p.m. He was starving but wasn't allowed to eat anything. He wanted to lick the bag of the Donna Bell's treats we had brought with us, but diabetic Irwin had to wait until 7:00 p.m. Then we waited a week for the results. We felt the same anxiety as always, maybe just a little less. We kept our fingers crossed. We realized that our journey was not over and would never really be, but we were focused on living and were OK. Irwin said, "I am so glad that I am alive and able to have a seven-hour day in the hospital."

Tuesday we took the subway to the Ortiz Funeral Home to attend the viewing of our friend Martha. She was part of our Pancreatic Support Group. She was soft-spoken and eloquent. Her story was more common than we wish. She couldn't have the Whipple surgery, which was a big problem, and she suffered through several unsuccessful chemo protocols and radiation. She was courageous in her battle against pancreatic cancer. She fought to live and prayed for a miracle, but this was not to be. I spoke to her each week during the past ten months, and we shared stories of our lives. We appreciated and supported one another. Her beautiful daughter, Helen, was gracious and lovely as she stood beside her mother's casket, comforting the guests. Martha was at peace at last. We met another person from the support group, Nancy, Carolyn's caregiver sister, at the funeral home, and she and Irwin looked at Martha and knew that but for the grace of God…well, you know the rest. Yes, pancreatic cancer continues to shape our lives in many ways.

On Wednesday, I was at the supermarket. I pretended, as I often did, that I was in Paris and was buying fresh fruit and vegetables. I bought Gatorade for Irwin to keep up his electrolytes. He drank a bottle each day. I spoke to the manager and told him that my husband was a cancer survivor and that I missed the summer prices, which were a dollar a bottle less.

The next day I was back at the market, and the fruit and produce man Eric, whom I had spoken with over the years, asked me, "How's your husband doing?" I looked at him surprised, and he said, "I overheard you talking to the manager yesterday."

I told Eric, "Irwin had pancreatic cancer surgery and six months of intensive chemotherapy; it's been one year since he finished his treatment."

Eric replied, "The Big Man upstairs had other plans for Irwin," and gave me a hug. Life goes on.

Thursday Irwin had an appointment to see Dr. Dixon, our foot doctor, as part of his ongoing diabetic care. As soon as he walked into the office, the doctor said, "I'm so glad to see you! My sixty-seven-year-old sister, who lives in California, was just diagnosed with pancreatic cancer and will have surgery soon. What can you tell me about the Whipple?"

Irwin gave him a lot of information and returned to the doctor's office with a draft copy of this book. The doctor hoped that he and the family would be able to visit his sister at Thanksgiving in six weeks. Irwin returned home and told me, "We must get this book published because people need to hear our story. People need hope." We know that there is a message in my words and that my book is important to anyone who faces a catastrophic life-threatening calamity.

Friday we were both called into school. We love these kids, and they were a diversion for us as we waited several days for the results of the tests and wondered if Dawn had heard anything.

Saturday Irwin had chemo brain, which is a side effect of all of the chemo. As a result some brain cells were damaged. It isn't a serious situation, but it's definitely annoying, because a person's memory is temporarily affected. Although it has been almost a full year since he finished treatment, he still occasionally has difficulty remembering the exact procedure for taking his eighteen pills, three finger pricks to check his sugar levels, and four insulin shots a day. I don't have chemo brain, but I am sometimes overwhelmed with thoughts in my head. Unfortunately Irwin's confusion could be life-threatening. For him to have survived the Whipple surgery and a chemo protocol and then, by mistake, almost slip into a diabetic coma was crazy.

Monday to Friday he was more regimented with his meds. However, during the weekends, he sleeps later and then got confused whether or not he had taken his insulin before lunch and then took it again after lunch, which caused his number to drop to forty-seven (normal is 120 to 150). He became disoriented and confused. Luckily I was in the living room and ran to him when he called. Dawn in the past, had told him not to worry about an occasional high sugar but that a low sugar could be deadly. Irwin felt badly because he got confused with his meds, so he slammed a few doors in frustration. The old (pre-metamorphosis) Irwin once in a while rears his ugly head, but this time it was short-lived. We tried to relax for the remainder of the weekend.

On Monday we heard from Dawn. We both held our breath. One phone call could change everything. She told us that he was cancer-free and that the infection in his liver that he'd had since last November (requiring the biopsy) was completely gone. Thank you, God, Dr. Fine, and Dawn—not necessarily in that order. Our tears were tears of happiness and joy. And life went on as we hugged each other. Irwin squeezed my hands so strongly that I winced in pain. Of course when I think of all that he has gone through, this hero (as Fred and Judy have called him), Irwin, gives me strength. I will never forget the courage he has exhibited during these past 20 months.

It was a beautiful, clear, sunny fall day in New York City. The leaves on Irwin's adopted tree in the garden between the two buildings where we live had started turning from green to bright yellow and orange. Irwin, Olive, now five, and I were on a crowded train in the subway, with Olive sitting on my lap. Not realizing and inadvertently, Olive rested her hand on my right breast and gently kept it there. A young twenty-something handsome man sitting across from us smiled quietly from ear to ear. Isn't life and living wonderful? It had been the worst of times and the best of times in that order, and we face the future with a smile.

ACKNOWLEDGEMENTS

For the readers of this book, I wish you good health and good luck.

Special thanks to the brilliant students and to my generous colleagues at Columbia Grammar and Prep School, especially Serena Depero and Suzy Mehler who showed me how to cut and paste, and upload my manuscript with my less than capable computer skills. Thanks to my team at Createspace who guided me through this unknown world of self-publishing.

I extend my gratitude to my friends and family who supported me during this project and offered advice and encouragement. Special friends and you know who you are, listened, made me laugh, and provided an outlet for me when I needed to vent.

My sons, Ryan and Darren, son–in–law Sam all lived this battle for PopPop's life. They always found the time in their busy lives to answer my questions and provide support and caring. My darlings, Maya and Olive give me the world with their love.

For Irwin there are still surprises after almost fifty years of marriage. Your strength, courage and grace when faced with the unthinkable came shining through the darkness. To quote Barry White's song, "You're my first. My last, my everything."